Encounters with Witchcraft

PRESS

AFRICAN-CARIBBEAN INSTITUTE

For
Judith von Daler Miller

BOOKS By Norman N. Miller

Kenya: The Quest for Prosperity

Wildlife, Wild Death: Land Use and Survival in Eastern Africa
(with Rodger Yeager)

AIDS in Africa: The Social and Policy Impact
(editor, with Richard Rockwell)

Faces of Change: Five Rural Societies in Transition
(general editor, film textbook)

Research in Rural Africa (editor)

FILMS Produced by Norman N. Miller

Faces of Change
26 film series funded by the National Science Foundation

Forgotten Farmers: Women and Food Security
United Nations, Food and Agricultural Organization

Encounters with Witchcraft

FIELD NOTES FROM AFRICA

Norman N. Miller

PRESS

AFRICAN-CARIBBEAN INSTITUTE

Published in the United States of America
State University of New York Press
www.sunypress.edu

Published in cooperation with the African-Caribbean Institute, Hanover, NH and
Nairobi, Kenya

© 2012 Norman N. Miller

Cover Art: power emblem from the Ekpe society, Banyang peoples in the Cameroon/
Nigeria border areas. Used by permission of the owners.
Cover and Text design: Carrie Fradkin, Lebanon, NH
Printed by Thomson-Shore

All individuals mentioned in the text are real people. Six names have been changed to
protect identities when necessary.

Photographs: All photographs (c) 2011 by Norman N. Miller unless otherwise noted.
Due to the in situ origin of these field photos some images are not of the best quality
and are included here for historical value. Permissions for all others will be found
starting on page 222 and are a continuation of the copyright page.

Library of Congress Cataloging-in-Publication Data

Miller, Norman N., 1933-
 Encounters with witchcraft : field notes from Africa / Norman N.
Miller.
     p. cm.
 Includes bibliographical references and index.
 ISBN 978-1-4384-4358-4 (pbk. : alk. paper) -- ISBN 978-1-4384-4357-7
(hardcover : alk. paper) 1. Witchcraft--Social aspects--Africa,
Sub-Saharan. I. Title.
 BF1584.A53M55 2012
 133.4'30967--dc23
                                          2011042635

10   9   8   7   6   5   4   3   2   1

CONTENTS

LIST OF MAPS

Prologue: First Encounter

My first experience with witchcraft in Africa occurred in March 1960 in Mombasa, Kenya, just as I stepped off the gangway of the MS *Inchanga* following a voyage from India. Next to the ship in a dockside kiosk I saw a newspaper with the headline, "European Geologist Attacked in Gogoland: Witchcraft Suspected." It was the story of a 22-year-old British geologist, William Hanning, who had been prospecting for minerals in a remote part of nearby Tanzania when by mistake he dug into a burial ground. He was believed to be a witch, disguised as a European, out to steal body parts and to destroy ancestral graves.

Those were my first moments on African soil and as I read the article in the shadow of the grimy freighter, the smell of fish and diesel oil blowing along the dock, hair began to stand up on the back of my neck. I was two years older than Hanning and until that point had naively planned to hitchhike across colonial East Africa. The story frightened me enough to stay in the city a few days and learn something about African witchcraft

At the port gate a customs officer told me about a library in a European settler's club in the old Arab quarter of Mombasa. When I found the stucco building, near the sixteenth-century Portuguese-built Fort Jesus, a huge British Union Jack fluttered over the doorway. Further on, off the club's veranda, two large *dhows* from Oman rode at anchor in the old harbor. Inside, a small, suspicious European desk clerk said that for a "temporary membership" I could use the library, the swimming "bath," and have meals as I wished. Then he paused.

"You're not a seaman are you? We don't take seamen. There is a drinking club that takes seamen on Nyali Road."

"Just a traveler," I said. "Just for the library."

I paid the fee and was shown into a lounge with wicker furniture, potted ferns and high windows open to the sea breeze. An old man snored in a rocking chair and two women read magazines on a nearby couch. Beyond was the small library with bookshelves reaching to the ceiling. The overall atmosphere was stultifying and only changed two hours later when a small crowd gathered for "sundowners" on the harbor veranda.

On that particular afternoon I learned that "witchcraft" was a set of beliefs *and* practices found in most of the developing world. A witch in Africa was seen as a *living* person with hidden powers to harm, not a spirit or ghost or ancestor. Concrete activities attributed to witches included using poisons, casting spells, uttering curses, and intimidating people with the threat of bewitchment—often for money. Witchcraft services could be hired and there was profit in healers protecting people who believed themselves bewitched. Laws against the practices were in place in nearly all African colonies and in British-controlled East Africa it was a crime to *claim* to be a witch, to *carry* paraphernalia for witchcraft or to *attack* anyone believed to be a witch. Most Africans loathed witchcraft and numerous anti-witchcraft movements had been launched across East and Central Africa, the larger ones often led by self-proclaimed witch-hunting prophets in semi-Christian sects.

Fort Jesus, Mombasa Kenya

One of the European settlers who used the library, the snoring man, was Peter Lavers, a retired headmaster from a missionary school in western Kenya. On the third day I watched him shuffle into the reading room and hang his pith helmet on a wall peg. We nodded and I decided to ask him if he had ever encountered a witchcraft case.

"Yes, many times," he said. "Among the blacks—my black staff." He then turned slightly red and began to sputter. "Despicable...despicable...an evil practice, sir! Not the business of civilized humans. Not the business of moral people."

He took a deep breath, searched for his handkerchief and wiped his mouth. Europeans, he said, with his index finger up in the air, were quite justified in colonizing Africa, not only to bring Christianity to the "savages," but to dispel witchcraft. It was the scourge of the continent, and blacks were very lucky that Europeans had come to save them... save them from their ignorance, disease *and* witchcraft.

"But there must be different kinds of practitioners," I said. "Healers, shamans, diviners, they are not all the same. They…."

"All the same," he hissed. "All are witch doctors, root doctors, bush doctors, rainmakers, even those who claim to prevent grasshopper attacks. All exploiters! Despicable, sir! Despicable!"

The two ladies on the nearby couch in the lounge nodded in agreement.

Over the next five days the books and journals in the library gave me a lot to think about. What was the origin of witchcraft? Did the claimed powers really work? Could it be there really were *spirits* out there, particularly "*evil spirits*"? Why did so much violence flow from modern cases of witchcraft? Were women always the main victims, the scapegoats?

The library also gave me an introduction to the region. East Africa consisted of Kenya, Tanganyika and Uganda, in those days all under British colonial rule. Tanganyika, later renamed Tanzania, had been a German colony until World War I, thereafter administered by the British as a League of Nations Mandated Territory. Uganda was a British protectorate, meaning limited settlement; Kenya, a colony in which European settlement was encouraged. The region I was about to cross was the size of western Europe and if my plans worked out I would

"All are witch doctors, root doctors, bush doctors, rainmakers…

see a coastal rainforest, grassland savannahs, agricultural highlands in Kenya, the densely populated Lake Victoria basin, fertile Uganda and the rainforests of the eastern Congo. There were 190 ethnic groups in East Africa including Maasai, Kikuyu, Baganda, Nyamwezi, and Kenya Somali. There were almost as many vernacular languages. Swahili was a trade language. Literacy in 1960 was estimated at around 40 percent, and all three countries were predominately rural, up to nearly 80 percent in Tanzania. The total population of the three countries in 1960 was estimated at twenty-four million.

Several authors tied witchcraft to poverty and when I was able to study the region's geography, I could see why. Most land in East Africa was poor, only around 10 percent of the region was arable, soil erosion was widespread and insect-borne and water-borne disease was endemic. Rainfall for much of the region was episodic, and mainly for that reason, the population was concentrated on the coasts, in the green belt of southern Kenya, around Lake Victoria, in the southern highlands of Tanzania and in southern Uganda.

I was also intrigued by the reported religious composition: Tanzania was one-third Moslem, one-third Christian and one-third traditional belief, where presumably witchcraft ideas found refuge. Kenya and Uganda were considered more Christian, but it was obvious even in those early reports, the mixing and meshing of ideas allowed most Africans to borrow from each of the faiths as their circumstances dictated. I came away from those library days with the conviction that witchcraft was deep within the social fabric, particularly in poor rural areas where health and education services had yet to penetrate. One author said witchcraft is a "floor of life" issue.

On the sixth day in Mombasa, at the dockside, I watched the *Inchanga* drop its lines and ease into the harbor with the help of a green tug. The Captain had let me sleep aboard while the *Inchanga* was in port and now I waited with my backpack to see the ship's departure. Suddenly, for some reason, I felt a deep sense of loneliness. I didn't want the ship to leave. I didn't want to be left behind. The feelings were sharp but they made no sense since I had just ridden the vessel from India and it was returning to Bombay. Trudging back into Mombasa I startled a dozing fruit vendor with my half shout: "Get over it. You're homesick. You're road-weary."

...witchcraft is a "floor of life" issue.

Kenya was the half-way point in a two-year journey that had begun in San Francisco. With college and a tour in the peacetime U.S. Air Force as a junior officer behind me, I had simply decided to go to the Orient and once there, to go on around the world. One hope was to find a mate, the perfect wife, whatever her nationality. The deeper truth was that I had no job and no idea of an occupation and at age twenty-four had simply given in to wanderlust. Prior to sailing on the *Inchanga,* I had been trekking in Nepal and India for six months. In fact "Mother India" had been a hot, hard classroom, teeming with humanity, dusty and dirty at my budget level. All the way across the Indian ocean I had looked forward to Africa, to what I envisioned as the vast green savannahs, the fresh air, the great natural beauty.

The next morning, just before I began hitchhiking up the unpaved, rock-strewn road toward Nairobi, I learned that William Hanning had died of his spear wounds. His body was being sent back to his parents in the Midlands of England.

A Look Ahead. Of course I did not know it in 1960, but East Africa would become my second home. After this first trip I came back to the United States for graduate studies in African politics and anthropology, as well as Swahili. Over the ensuing years I journeyed to Africa twenty-six times, spending a total of twelve years on the ground. I was married in Nairobi and initially found work in the region as a university teacher, journalist and filmmaker. In the later years I was able to serve as an adviser to the three African governments, plus several UN agencies. Although I kept notes of my experiences and did a great deal of research on the topic, witchcraft was a secondary interest until I began to write this account in 2005.

1

The Colonial Days

1960

James Kirkman, archaeologist, Ft. Jesus, Mombasa, Kenya
Hamisi Ali, caretaker, Cheke III stone site, Tanzania
Walter Reece, District Commissioner, Kondoa, Tanzania
Mary Leakey, Olduvai Gorge, Tanzania
Samuel Mbonye, artist, Kampala, Uganda
Walter Baumgartel, gorilla researcher, Kisoro, Uganda
Ruben, gorilla tracker, Kisoro, Uganda
Jean Pierre Hallet, friend of Ituri Pygmies, Congo

After landing in Mombasa, my first trip across East Africa was by road through Kenya and Tanzania, across Uganda, into the Eastern Congo, and then north through the Sudan. These were peaceful times in the region, and I was able to trek in good weather, use rural buses and find rides with traders or truckers and occasionally missionaries. In fact, it was the good luck on the road that was so different from India and most of Asia. African truckers took me home to meet their families, Indian *duka* (store) keepers gave me shelter in their shops at night, and an array of English and Belgian "colonials," mostly ranchers or farm managers, were glad to have company on the road.

On a desolate stretch of road that ran through the middle of the huge Tsavo game park I flagged down an oil truck, saw the African driver nod, and climbed the ladder to the passenger's seat.

"We never see Europeans flagging us down, they all have cars," said the burly trucker, Judson Mutiso. "But we drivers, none of us picks up Africans unless they wave shillings. Sure, Bwana, when they pay, even I will stop. I will pick them for sure."

Then, without a trace of rancor, he added, "But you Europeans... your white face is your passport. No one will pass you by." He paused to shift gears and after the grinding stopped, Judson Mutiso looked over and smiled. "You are welcome in my country, Mister Norman. Africa will take care of you."

As events unfolded, he was right, most of the time.

Author with wreath of flowers for completing climb of Mt. Kilimanjaro, 1960.

I was enthralled by the human landscape on the Kenya coast, the melange of African, Indian, Arab and European. The things I remember most about traveling inland were the vast open spaces, the shouts and waves of herd boys, the spectacular birdlife and the majestic mountains that rose abruptly from the grasslands—especially Kilimanjaro and Meru. The wildlife sanctuaries at Tsavo, Serengeti, Amboseli and Murchison Falls were still largely undiscovered by tourists. Mt. Kilimanjaro had a high crown of snow, and when I struggled up the mountain in April of 1960 on a five-day climb and signed the book at Gilman's Point, my signature was only the 32nd of that year. Nearby, Mary and Louis Leakey had just discovered *Zinjanthropus*, the 1.7 million-year-old hominid, at Olduvai Gorge and, because of their work, East Africa was increasingly seen as the "birthplace of man."

Before leaving Mombasa, in order to learn more about witchcraft I spent time with Dr. James Kirkman, curator of the Ft. Jesus museum. He was an Englishman who had been in East Africa since World War

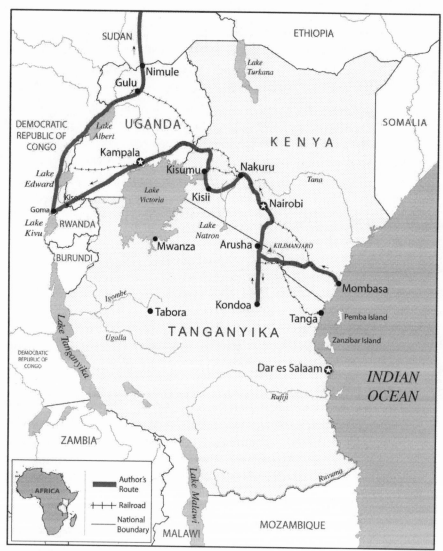

Map of East Africa showing author's route, 1960.

II, a well-respected archaeologist who specialized in the Islamic history of the Swahili coast. I made an appointment and found him in a dank office under the north rampart of the fort. He greeted me with pipe in hand and a slight stutter and then apologized for the dank smell.

"Back in 1800 this room was either a fish house or a...a dungeon where the prisoners pissed in the corner. You should have smelled it last year," he laughed. "This pipe is my defense."

When I told him I had come from Asia on a long "walkabout," that I needed advice on where to go and what to see, and that I had a new interest in witchcraft and witch doctors, he waved me to a chair and immediately put his finger up in the air.

"Forget 'witch doctor,'" he said. "It's a journalistic term. It confuses things. For Africans, for all of us here, a witch is evil, a doctor is good. There is really no such thing as 'witch doctor.' Swahili distinguishes between a good healer, *mganga*, and a bad 'witch,' *mchawi*." He watched me scribbling notes and patiently spelled out the Swahili words, then relit his pipe and smiled, "How can I help?"

I told him my plan was to spend four months traveling in East Africa, that I wanted to see several archaeological sites and museums, and two or three game parks, to try to get to know rural Africans, and that the witchcraft business was a new interest. I thought I might someday study anthropology, and I wanted to know more about the beliefs.

"Should I talk to missionaries, teachers, storekeepers, policemen?" I asked.

"Not missionaries," he said, shaking his head. "Not if you want unbiased information. They have the same kind of ideas as the Africans who believe in witchcraft. African spirits or Christian devils, all the same things. New missionaries out here don't know anything. Old timers? Chances are they are rabid, almost irrational on the subject. Most see witchcraft as the devil's work, the belief of heathens. Especially the fundamentalists from your southland, those 'born-again' people." He tamped his pipe and thought for a moment.

"African teachers would be good to talk to, and local government officers and local magistrates in the districts you pass through. Anti-witchcraft

> "Forget 'witch doctor,'" he said. "It's a journalistic term."

laws give them a lot of trouble. Not African police or constables—they won't talk. Sometimes they won't even investigate a witchcraft case."

"Won't investigate?" I asked.

"For fear of revenge, afraid their families might get poisoned or attacked by the witch they are investigating. Fear like that is everywhere. That's why most of the violent attacks against 'witches' are by gangs or vigilante groups." He waved two fingers in the air when he said "witches."

"Why the quotes?" I asked.

"Witches don't exist," he answered, "not the way Africans and most others imagine them. True, plenty of people claim to be witches, and plenty confess to witchcraft to save themselves. Plenty more make money as healers diagnosing witchcraft or witch-hunters. But the powers people think 'witches' have, that's rubbish. Witches are imaginary. There are no witches—no unicorns, no flying dragons out there either. No one turns a cousin into a crocodile. It damn well can't be done."

Kirkman patiently defined several terms that dealt with witchcraft. I wrote as fast as I could.

"If you are serious about this business," he said, "start a glossary. Right, do a glossary. Look up *juju* and *muti*, too."

Dr. Kirkman had an African teacher and five students waiting to see him, so he gave me a few things to read and we agreed to meet the next afternoon. One article was a translation of an old Portuguese chronicle that described what the Europeans thought witchcraft was in the early sixteenth century. It made me wonder about the origin of early witchcraft ideas. When we sat down again, I had my question ready.

"What about the roots of witchcraft?" I said. "The origins. How far back can you trace these African beliefs?"

Kirkman stared at me. Then he slowly began to stutter and shake his head.

"I...I have never heard that question asked before," he stammered. "Witchcraft is too soft a topic for archaeology. It's hard to...to get beliefs out of the ground."

KIRKMAN'S GLOSSARY

Diviner   One who explains a mystery, reveals hidden truths, a soothsayer or foreteller, believed to have magical powers.

Evil eye   The belief that looking askance, staring or prolonged glances, particularly toward a child, can cause sickness.

Juju   Venerated object or medicine in West Africa; also a term for witchcraft.

Muti   Poison or dangerous potions in southern Africa; general term for witchcraft.

Oath   In East African context, an enforced promise, often under threat of bewitchment.

Ordeal   Enforced drinking of concoctions or other physical trials to prove innocence of witchcraft.

Shaman   Healer, diviner, one believed able to enter the spirit world to discover reasons for illness or misfortune. Term used in southern Africa among hunter/gatherers. Origin in Siberia.

Sorcerer   Individual with acquired or learned powers to do malicious acts, a technician.

Spirit medium   One who is able to communicate with the spirit world.

Uchawi   Swahili for witchcraft; Mchawi, a witch; Wachawi, witches.

Voodoo. From *voodum* in West Africa, a spirit belief system in Haiti involving ancestor worship, rituals, candles, special foods, a mixing of African and Caribbean beliefs. Has parallels to witchcraft.

Witch   A living person *believed* to have innate powers to do evil (compare Sorcerer). Some ethnic groups believe a person may not be conscious of being a witch.

Witchcraft   A set of beliefs *and* practices, a social process, a system of thought that lacks the dogma and trappings of organized religion. A belief in the power of evil.

Witch-finder   Those who hunt for witches and often name or accuse someone of witchcraft. Witch-finding may include forms of "cleansing" such as head shaving of alleged witches, and other forms of exorcism. Extensive witch-hunting movements occurred across central Africa, including southern Tanzania between 1910-1960's.

The Makapansgat stone found in a cave in the northern Transvaal, South Africa (6 cm wide), is dated at 2.5 to 3.0 million years.

The Great God of Sefar
An early rock art image from Tassili Massif in the central Sahara (Algeria) depicts mysterious spirit beings and strange animal forms, similar to modern witchcraft images in East Africa. (Poznan Archeological Museum, Poznan, Poland)

He sat looking dejected, then suddenly brightened. "OK, if you see witchcraft as one specific belief in early religious ideas, like one stick in a bundle, then you at least know the context. It is certain there were very early ideas of spirits, and a spirit world is seen in cave art for at least 25,000 years. The idea of life after death goes back much farther—with the tools, weapons, and food buried with people for use in the next world. In early cave art there are also images that hint at creation ideas, a distant creator—for some, a sun god. So we know a little about early beliefs."

"Hard evidence of a witch, of witchcraft ideas? The first images?" I asked.

Kirkman again looked perplexed. "Earliest images? I...ah...I don't know. The carved wooden images, the masks are all gone, rotted centuries ago. Bronze, the Nok masks, still exist, but they are from the early Christian era."

He still looked perplexed, but then he jumped from his swivel chair, hurried across the room and began rummaging in an old file cabinet.

"Look at this," he said, pulling out a tattered black and white picture. He seemed to have found an old friend.

"This guy is bad. Really evil. It is the Makapansgat stone, from a South African cave, found with tools of proto-humans who lived two and a half million years ago. Is that old enough for you? It looks like a witch to me. It may have been what our ancestors thought witches were like. It at least suggests they had aesthetic ideas. They brought it back to their cave from a jasperite site 30 miles away. And look at this other image, some spirit beings from the Central Sahara. Don't they look like witchcraft ideas? Here is another image. Is that witchcraft?"

Kirkman then put on the brakes. "Of course this guy, this stone— it only proves proto-humans had a stone in their cave that today *we* think looks evil, or that there are ancient images that look like a spirit of some kind. None of this is hard evidence of early witchcraft practice. Your best bet is with the paleolinguists."

"Paleolinguists?" I said. "How do they prove witchcraft?"

"They trace words in early languages. A man named Malcolm Guthrie is the guru. The words for 'witch,' 'witchcraft' and 'bewitch' he reports are found in proto-Bantu, the language family that was around before Bantu—called the *Benue Kwa*. Bantu emerged around 3500 BC in West Africa. The word 'witchcraft' would have come across Africa with the Bantu migrations. A few pre-historians claim to see evidence of witchcraft in language and ritual items at around 5000 BC ."

"What is your view?" I asked. "When did witchcraft come on the scene in Africa?"

"My guess is these ideas started when ancient hunter-gatherers settled and began to domesticate crops and build villages. For Africa that would have been around 9500 BC . There was a transition, when people no longer lived in hunting and gathering bands of thirty or so individuals. When they settled into groups of over a hundred, they needed a leader, a chief or priest who had authority, some kind of control. I think witchcraft was needed by leaders to accuse someone of evil, of being a traitor; they'd call him a witch. I think witchcraft was an early form of power and control, of very early government."

The next day when I came to say good-bye to James Kirkman in his dungeon, I asked him where I might see some of the cave art he talked about, where I might get hints of early witchcraft ideas.

"Try the stone paintings at Kondoa," he said. "You'll find some interesting images… They were hunter-gatherers."

He started to stutter, so he lit his pipe again and waved the smoke

"When did witchcraft come on the scene in Africa?"

away. The faint smell of fish was still there. "If…if…if you find something interesting," he said with a broad smile, "write me a letter. Hell, write me anyway."

Ten days later, after my struggle up Mt. Kilimanjaro, I stepped off a rural bus at a sign that read "Cheke III Rock Site." It was some 220 miles south of Kilimanjaro, on the Arusha-Dodoma road, a desolate, wind-swept place with only a sign and a track leading into thick bush. The driver and one of the wizened old men I had made friends with on the bus both motioned me ahead.

"*Sawa, sawa* (OK, OK)," they shouted, pointing down the trail. "No *simbas*, no lions."

In spite of their assurances, I picked up a stout stick and hurried down the track looking over the wavering grass for anything that moved. The day was still hot, there was a dusty haze in the air and it seemed like an uneasy, forbidding place. In less than a mile I began to see large rocky outcrops, and soon another sign announced "Cheke III." At the end of the track was a thornbush fence that stretched around a cluster of boulders. Inside the enclosure was a grass lean-to where a caretaker dozed in the shade. Beyond him a steep hill with cave openings rose abruptly from the plains. There were goats on the hillside.

The caretaker's name was Hamisi Ali, and with the help of my Swahili dictionary, I learned he had a *shamba* (farm) nearby, that he was Muslim, and that he had only one wife, plus three daughters and a son. He took pains to tell me that he very much wanted a second wife and was saving for the bride price. In the visitors' book he gave me to sign the signature above mine was six weeks old.

Hamisi's job was to guard the rock paintings, which meant cutting the brush back and keeping the goats from licking the rocks for traces of salt. He used thornbushes for a fence against the goats, keeping the brush in place with a row of stones he had painted white. After I had paid a two-shilling fee, he led me to one of the rock paintings situated under a low-hanging ledge. It was near the ground, only three feet off the sand.

"No simbas,
no lions."

Author's rough sketches of Cheke III. Redrawn by Susan Whelihan.

"*Zamani, watu wa fupi* (In the past, people were short)," he said as I found a place in the shade to sit and sketch the figures.

Sometime later I noticed him watching the horizon and followed his gaze to where small puffs of dust were kicked up by the wind. In the shimmering heat, they looked like tiny people moving quietly across the savannah. It was an eerie moment, as if we were looking back in time, seeing ancient humans en route to a ceremony. The only sound was the wind around the huge boulders, the rustling of the bushes and then a distant birdcall.

"*Shetani* (spirits, ghosts, witches)," Hamisi said, seeing my gaze.

I remembered his earlier description of the small ancient cave painters and looked up the word for "short."

"*Shetani fupi*," I said, holding my hand three feet off the ground.

He nodded and smiled. He had seen the dust devils before, but

Author's sketches of figures from Kondoa area stone art. Redrawn by Susan Whelihan.

probably not imagined them as the ancient people who had painted the rocks centuries earlier. Hamisi sauntered off to doze in the shade but after a while came back with typed notes about the Cheke III site, plus an article from an archaeological journal.

I learned there was still a mystery about when and why Stone Age people painted here. Painting sticks have been found in 19,000-year-old soil deposits, although most evidence points to human activity 10,000-12,000 years ago. The artists were hunter-gatherers, but no one knows why they painted as they did. The many animal depictions suggest more vegetation was here then and that the area was a ceremonial meeting place where small bands came together for hunting rituals. Elands are important animals in the paintings.

The article compared the Kondoa paintings to similar rock art in South Africa where medicine-induced trances, rainmaking and other

A Sandawe ceremonial shield (circa 1920s) carries decorations similar to those found in early stone art in the Kondoa region of Tanzania. (National Museum, Dar es Salaam, Tanzania)

magical activities are depicted. Kondoa may have been an open-air religious site, some kind of Stone Age cathedral. One of Hamisi's reprints showed a nineteenth-century Sandawe shield with decorations suggesting a tie with the earlier rock art.

After I had sketched several rock paintings, and hiked across the area, I wandered back to the gate to find that Hamisi had tied my backpack to the carrier on his bicycle. He pulled the gate closed behind him and blocked it with a stone.

"*Hakuna mbuzi* (no goats)," he said to the gate.

As we set off, Hamisi seemed to know I found Kondoa's Cheke III a mysterious place, made more so by the emptiness and the dust devils blowing in the distance. We walked along in silence and then waited on the road. Eventually a pickup truck came racing over a distant hill creating a rooster-tail of dust. Hamisi stepped out into the road and held up his hand. At what seemed like the last possible moment, the driver slammed on his brakes and covered us in dust. I was waved into the front seat and my pack placed carefully in the back.

"*Kwaheri shetani* (farewell spirit)," Hamisi said, clasping my outstretched hand with both of his. The driver was totally bewildered, but Hamisi didn't care. He pointed toward Kondoa town and simply said: "*Hoteli.*"

After a night in Kondoa, in a tiny room freshly painted light blue, with a sagging bed and a mosquito net with at least three holes, I decided to follow James Kirkman's advice and try to learn how the British colonial government handled witchcraft cases.

The Kondoa District Commissioner's office, called a *boma* (fort), was near the edge of town. It was also surrounded by thornbushes, but in this case had a gatehouse and a guard. He motioned me around the pole that swung up and down, and pointed up the hill to a U-shaped building. Near the front steps the Union Jack fluttered on a wooden pole. A second guard in a khaki uniform dozed in a canvas chair, a carbine leaning against the wall. To my surprise, when I approached he suddenly jumped up, stamped one foot, and saluted.

"Sir!" he said in a loud voice and for a split second we stared at each other. He then stepped back, opened the office door and pointed to a clerk sorting mail.

The guard's stamping must have been heard behind a green door marked "District Commissioner." It opened, and a tall, sandy-haired European strolled out. I guessed him to be in his late thirties.

"Good God, a visitor!" he exclaimed. "First one in a week!" He was smiling and holding out his hand. "I'm Reece, Walter David Reece to be exact. I'm Acting."

"Acting?" I said, after introducing myself.

"Ah yes—you're a Canadian or something strange. The DC is on home leave for three months. I'm standing in for him. My proper post is Iringa. Here, I'm the Acting District Commissioner."

Walter Reece was to become a lifelong friend. We would later teach together at the University of Dar es Salaam, do research together, and visit one another over the years. He was fourteen years my senior, an Oxford graduate who had been posted to Somalia as a military officer at the end of World War II. He served there in the administration in peacetime and then was transferred to the Tanganyika colonial service in Iringa. There, at the Iringa provincial hospital he met a young English nurse.

"We married in 'far off Africa' and her mother has yet to forgive me," Reece said as he poured tea. "She is in Iringa with our girls…two girls."

Nothing I had imagined about officious colonial officers fit Walter Reece. He was open and good-natured to a fault. He loved Africa, especially the safari life, and had an obvious respect for the Africans he worked with, particularly the elders. Like Kirkman, his only prejudices were white missionaries, mainly American Southern Baptists, because of their proselytizing.

In colonial Tanganyika, because of the remoteness and long distances between government posts, district offices usually had small guesthouses for official visitors. In order that I might explore the surrounding area, I was invited to use Kondoa's guesthouse as long as it was not needed for an official visitor.

"What do you want to be?" Reece laughed as he signed me in. "Road engineer, pans and dams man, tsetse fly officer?"

Like James Kirkman, Walter Reece was an instinctive teacher and he soon clarified my misunderstanding of the dust devils at the Cheke III rock site. *Shetani* is not a term for a witch, but rather the Islamic idea of a spirit or jinn, often a prankster, more like a ghost, and a *shetani* could be either good or bad. Later, when I asked him how the colonial administration dealt with witchcraft cases, he thought about the question for quite a while.

"OK, let me give you an example of how these witchcraft beliefs can work, how they can cause havoc. Have you heard of the lion-men cases? They were reported in England, perhaps not in America."

Reece explained that many cultures in East Africa and the Congo believe in transformation myths, that some humans, using witchcraft, could turn themselves into animals or turn animals into humans. Before World War II, in Singida District just to the south of us, there were killings that looked like lion maulings, the victims slashed with claws. In the late 1940s, an outbreak of killings terrified the region and began nearly two years of investigation by the colonial police. Eventually it was learned that the killers were assassins, paid to start political terror campaigns, to sell protection and carry out revenge killings. The actual murders were done by drugged, often demented, young men who were kept by handlers. "Lion-men" were treated as animals, given raw meat, tethered and forced to sleep in hyena holes. They were armed with both knives and lion claws attached to heavy gloves. Most killings were ambushes in thickets, the habitat of lions.

The murders terrified thousands of villagers, not only because of the grisly killings, but because the instigators spread rumors that the lions were controlled by witches, and that some humans could transform themselves into lions. Protective medicines and amulets were sold, which Reece thought might have created a side business and prolonged the terror.

"Sure, some people made money on the widespread fear," he said. "No doubt about it."

After investigating nearly 200 incidents, the colonial authorities brought 30 individuals to court. Six cases were tried, all with multiple defendants. Twenty-two people were found guilty, eleven hanged.

"Frankly, witchcraft cases are nightmares."

Eleven others avoided death on appeal. Those convicted included the male "handlers" of the "lion-men," some of the actual killers, and several women who had contracted for the murders of their husbands. The reign of terror was based on the belief that witchcraft could be used to turn someone into a lion.*

Walter Reece also knew a lot about the anti-witchcraft laws because his duties included serving as a magistrate at the district court. "Frankly, witchcraft cases are nightmares," he said. "People kill suspected witches because they believe they themselves have been bewitched, or that their child has been killed by a witch. In every murder case I have ever seen the defendant, the killer, claims he or she was bewitched. If the family can hire someone to advise them, they usually enter a plea of self-defense or insanity because of witchcraft."

"Does it work?" I asked. "Does believing yourself bewitched equal insanity?"

"Not usually," Reece replied. "At the district level of court, there is usually a guilty verdict."

"Then what happens?" I asked.

"If found guilty of murder, they are sentenced to hang. Then an appeal is entered, and sent to the provincial level. If sustained as guilty, the case is sent to the Governor in Council. That's the final appeal."

"Then?" I continued.

"Nearly always, in capital cases, the Governor sends a district officer back to the village of the condemned person—to talk to the elders."

"I don't understand," I said. "Your colonial legal system puts the African through a murder trial under colonial law, finds him guilty, then your Governor sends the case back to the village elders for a retrial?"

"Not a retrial," Reece said defensively. "Just a check on the condemned person's reputation. Remember a lot of people think killing a witch is a good idea, that the man, sometimes a woman, did a public service."

"What usually happens?" I asked.

Reece thought for a while, as if he were about to reveal a colonial secret. "OK...true, it is a bit of a dual system. We send a European district officer back out to the village to sit with the elders and ask if the sentence is justified."

* From the beginning authorities believed the murders were political, because of similar killings across Lake Tanganyika in the Congo. Those lion-men cases were carried out by Africans who had lost their land to Christian mission stations, the violence directed against African Christians who had been given land near the missions. British authorities also looked for parallels in the "leopard cults" of West Africa, because of their violent political activities.

I nodded to encourage him.

"It is not talked about in this way in the colonial service, but in all the capital cases I know, when the elders think the man was bad, really evil, and that he should swing, they hang him. When the elders report the condemned man was a good person, and the case involved a crime of passion, the governor commutes to a jail sentence…usually of some years."

"A dual system," I exclaimed, as if I had found a great truth. "How can your legal Lords in London justify a dual system?"

I thought Reece would argue, but he didn't.

"Simple," he said. "It keeps the peace, prevents unrest and keeps us from hanging good people. Remember our colonial predecessors around here, the Germans? They wouldn't fool around like this. There was summary justice for murder, with or without witchcraft pleas. It was usually quick. A firing squad. Most often in front of all the local chiefs as a way to teach them German justice. It worked—there was very little theft in those years."

The next day I was able to ride along with the district water engineer, an Asian named Hamid Khan, who was on a one-day safari to find new water sites. He hoped to drill for water and build earthen pans, backed up by small dams to help cattle survive in times of drought. At one point we stopped and he talked to a group of men in Swahili about where a dam might go. They were the Sandawe, the people Kirkman mentioned who spoke a form of the Khoisan language and whose grandfathers carried shields with ancient decorations. The men talked to Khan in Swahili, but when they were speaking together I heard the distinct clicks of the ancient Khoisan. I told Hamid Khan that I was fascinated by the way the men spoke because it was a hint of the oldest languages ever known, thought to have developed 40,000 years ago right here in East Africa. He gave me a shrug.

"I don't know about their language, but their women are very passionate. Wild, just wild. No. Let me correct that. They are shy in the day, but wild in the night."

When I was dropped at the guesthouse, there was a book with a note on the doorstep. Reece had found an article about the conflicts

"…Their women…They are shy in the day, but wild in the night."

colonial officers had with "witch-finders." I was also invited for tea, or a drink if it was past six o'clock.

When we met we sat on his porch with cold beers. I gave him a report on the day, then asked about the article he had left for me. It concerned witch-hunting. "How do you government folks handle the witch-finders? Don't they help keep the peace?"

"Depends on the situation," Reece said. "In cases involving violence or unrest caused by the witch-hunters, there is prompt action. We use the police, break up crowds, make arrests. But when violence is not an issue, a lot of colonial officers allow small-scale witch-finders to operate. They can help reduce the general fear of witchcraft."

"Are there witch-finders all over East Africa?" I asked.

"Among agriculturalists, any Bantu village can launch a witch-hunt, usually through a local healer or diviner. There have been big movements across southern Tanganyika and many of these people push religious messages and claim to be prophets. Around here most are just local healers. As I said, they can be useful in keeping the peace."

Reece got up and came back with two more beers, plus an envelope, then sat and put his feet on the railing.

"Part of the problem is the missionaries. Most see all witch-finders or healers as evil, as tools of the devil. A lot of them won't let healers into their church, and will destroy a healer's kit whenever they can. Some of these people are really misinformed because healers do a lot of good things. Let me show you two pictures I got from a researcher named Gus Liebenow who was working near the coast."

The next day, before I left Kondoa, Reece wanted to clarify his view on missionaries.

"They do a lot of good," he admitted. "Their schools, the health work, some teach farming techniques, bee-keeping, and other things. The Catholic 'white fathers' still go out on bicycles, they go miles in the sun to teach and say mass."

"You have changed your tune!" I exclaimed.

"A bit maybe—because there are all kinds of church people, some like saints. Others are really racists who won't let Africans into their gardens without ringing a bell. Some of the fundamentalists

A missionary and an African assistant burn a healer's paraphernalia believed to be used for witchcraft, at a mission station in Mtwara District, southern Tanzania. (J. Gus Liebenow collection)

The items include a large woven basket with medicinal leaves, flywhisks as power symbols, wooden rattles with string figures, and small dark gourds for medicinal powders. (J. Gus Liebenow collection)

see sin and Satan everywhere, particularly if a witchcraft case arises. A lot of the African sects that have broken away from mainline Christian churches actually use witchcraft ideas in their churches and do witch-hunts. Huge numbers! You'll see them in Kenya and Uganda. In fact a lot of them use witch-hunting as a reason to exist, as a way to recruit members."

Before I could understand more about the breakaway churches, my ride—the government's northbound supply truck—was ready to leave. Reece walked me to the supply shed and introduced me to the driver, who took my pack to the back of the truck.

"Good hunting," Reece smiled as we shook hands. He then said essentially the same thing that James Kirkman had said three weeks earlier: "If you learn something interesting out there, send me a letter."

Later that day the truck dropped me at a seedy "guesthouse" in Arusha, the supply town for the Serengeti and Ngorogoro wildlife areas. After a mosquito-filled night and a fried egg breakfast, I found a local bus going north toward the Kenya border. I wanted to visit the *Zinjanthropus* site at Olduvai Gorge and, by the time we reached the crossroad to Olduvai, I was friends with two Africans on the bus who worked for Louis and Mary Leakey—one a cook and another a worker on the excavation. They were on a supply run and, at the Olduvai road, a camp Land Rover was waiting. I helped transfer the boxes of food and caught a ride to the excavation.

At that time of year, Olduvai Gorge was a long, dry, parched valley on the western side of the Eastern Rift Valley, which runs through Kenya and Tanzania. Olduvai had been investigated in 1913 for fossil remains by Hans Reck and again, in 1932, by Reck and young Louis Leakey, a Kenya-born archaeologist. In 1935, Mary and Louis Leakey set up camp here and began systematically collecting artifacts, animal bones and fossils.

At Olduvai, I found several canvas tents near the parking area and, further on, a work tent with the side-flaps rolled up. Inside, Mary

Leakey was at a table strewn with artifacts, talking intently with two African assistants. When I was introduced by the cook, she immediately rose to shake hands, brushed the dust from her khaki skirt, and waved me to a canvas chair.

"Good, oh good," she said with a broad smile. "An excuse for lunch and word from the outside world."

In due course it was agreed that, since I was not there to work on the dig, I should have lunch, have a good "look about," and after tea take the mail and a box of artifacts with one of the drivers to Nairobi.

Over a lunch of sandwiches, fruit and tea, I learned that Mary Leakey had discovered *Zinjanthropus* on July 17, 1959. The find was a well-preserved cranium of a 1.75 million-year-old male that she and Louis Leakey named "Nutcracker Man." They called the discovery *Zinjanthropus boisei*, "Zinj" for the Arabic term for East Africa, "anthropus" for ape-human. "Boisei" was for Charles Boise, the philanthropist who supported the work at the time.

"Why 'Nutcracker Man'?" I asked as we hiked along a path to where a crew was digging.

"These people had big teeth with thick enamel," she said, "and a diet of hard nuts and seeds and roots. The ground cover then was full of vegetation, not so dry, a lot more to eat, more animals to hunt. I see this place as a great refrigerator, a great food store. The easy food, I think, was the reason these creatures, or their ancestors, wandered from the rainforests." *

In Nairobi, after I dropped the mail, I spent time trying to get a visa for the Sudan, which turned out to be a long process, and collecting information on Uganda and the Eastern Congo. It was also in Nairobi that I learned witchcraft beliefs could have a lot of social applications. The Mau Mau rebellion was one. Although Kenya was peaceful at that time, the Mau Mau land war that had raged across the country's central highlands six years before was still a vivid memory.

Witchcraft threats were used extensively by Mau Mau leaders to terrorize recruits into submission and to keep them from breaking

* In the years since 1960, Mary Leakey's discovery has been renamed *Paranthropus boisei,* one of a species that lived in both the Pliocene and the Pleistocene epochs, from about 1.2 million to about 2.6 million years ago. Another *Paranthropus* find, found by H. Mutya and Richard Leakey at Koobi Fora near Lake Turkana in Kenya in 1969, encouraged Richard Leakey to argue that *Paranthropus* was the first hominid to use stone tools.

their oaths of allegiance. Mau Mau propaganda claimed the leaders had witchcraft powers, which could enable them to exact hideous consequences for anyone disloyal to the movement.*

The power of the witchcraft threats was particularly evident after the combat subsided. When I was in Nairobi, hundreds of hard-core Mau Mau were in British detention camps, refusing to denounce the violence or recant their original oaths to oppose the colonial government and, in some cases, to kill a European. Mau Mau violence was dismissed by the British authorities as a nasty rebellion, but seen by African nationalists as a legitimate effort for independence and statehood.

Mau Mau leaders overprinted and circulated East African colonial stamps to undermine British authorities. (Larry Hausman Collection)

---

* I learned the Mau Mau rebellion was a land war staged against the British colonial regime by Africans of central Kenya, mainly the Kikuyu, Embu and Meru peoples. The problem began in the 1920s when a great deal of fertile land was taken by Europeans for farms and ranches. This preempting, plus population growth, led to periodic African protests, several instigated by an African nationalist, Harry Thuku. The freedom movement gained further ground after World War II, partially led by African soldiers who had fought for the British in Burma. Historians believe it was this combat that helped awaken nationalistic feelings among returning black soldiers, particularly those who had seen the vulnerability of the British in combat with the Japanese.

In Kenya, the combat was basic jungle warfare, mainly through hit-and-run raids by the Mau Mau, often against African villages deemed loyal to the British. Fewer than one hundred Europeans were killed. The Mau Mau lost 11,503 and their actions killed over 1,800 Africans loyal to the British. Jomo Kenyatta, later the first President of Kenya, was arrested early in the campaign and charged with leading the Mau Mau. Although the evidence was circumstantial, he was found guilty of sedition and jailed by the colonial government in the remote northern desert of Kenya.

In the 1959–1960 era, protesters demanding political freedom for Kenya used witchcraft images to draw attention to the issue outside a constitutional conference at Lancaster House in London. (Hutton-Deutsch Collection/ Corbis Images, HU055559)

After leaving Nairobi, I crossed the Rift Valley, worked briefly on a European farm near Naivasha, then hiked or rode local buses into Uganda. Along the main road, outside Kampala, I encountered a man creating an art form that I had never seen before. He used crushed paper and tinfoil to create small figures that depicted spirits, some in animal or human form. He was reluctant to talk about the work until his grandson bounded into the stall. From the boy I learned that the pieces were good-luck charms, protective symbols, and "spirit guards" to put by a front door or near a baby bed.

"Can they protect against witchcraft?" I asked.

"All of them," the old man announced before his grandson could answer. He picked up some of the silver spears, a doll with a paper hat, and another figure made of foil and put them out for display.

"Who gives them the protective power?" I asked, expecting to hear something about ancestors, or spirits of the homestead.

"He does," the grandson said. "He is a healer. He has magical powers that will protect you. The figures can protect you in any way he says they will. He has the power."

The old man put his finger over the boy's mouth.

"They will only protect, but they do not point out witches. It is against the law to name witches."

It struck me the old man thought I was investigating him.

"I'm not from Uganda," I said. "I don't mind if these objects name witches, if that's their job."

He seemed relieved and began to lay out more of the art. He then agreed to have the objects photographed if I would show them to friends in America. "I will be here," he said. "Tell them to find me: Samuel Mbonye on Jinja Road. I will be here."

In Kampala, Uganda I stayed at the Makerere University guesthouse, to do laundry and talk to African students and to learn as much as possible about western Uganda and the Congo. A British anthropologist, Audrey Richards, not only took an interest in my experiences in the Orient, but on three afternoons shared her knowledge of the cultures I was about to encounter. When we came to the topic of witchcraft, she suggested I visit a non-Bantu community.

Roadside art objects made by Samuel Mbonye from wood and tinfoil, sold for protection against witchcraft on the Jinja Road near Kampala, Uganda. (Author's collection)

"Go see the Pygmies," she said. "See how they use witchcraft, then compare what you learn to the nearby Bantu farmers. You will learn some very interesting things about human adaptation." I decided that was a good idea, a chance to learn more about a hunter-gatherer culture, possibly similar to the Sandawe I had met with Mr. Khan in Kondoa.

A week later, while crossing lush, verdant southern Uganda on a isolated stretch of road beyond Kabele, I hiked past a man sitting with a crossbow on his lap, apparently resting from hunting birds. The bow was loosely loaded, and four other arrows lay on the grass next to him. He was about fifty, small and wiry, with bare feet and tattered pants and splatters of mud caked on his clothes. Our eyes met. I nodded and thought I detected a nod in return. My camera was on my shoulder and I slipped it off, pointed to it and said in Swahili "*sawa-sawa?*" (OK, OK?) Again, I thought I got a nod. I lifted the camera, pointed and clicked the shutter.

"Instantly there was a scream of anger"

Instantly there was a scream of anger, then a stream of expletives recognizable in any language. In a split second, the arrow was fixed, the bow brought straight up, held out at arm's length and pointed straight at my chest.

I will never forget the look in his eyes. They were stone cold, very detached. As I began repeating "*sawa-sawa* (OK, OK), *salaama, salaama* (peace, peace)," I felt like an animal caught in a headlight. I was sweating and my head was pounding only on the left side. I could not believe what was happening, or what he was doing.

Some instinct told me to get lower to the ground. I squatted slowly with my hands up, until my knees touched the ground, then carefully laid the camera in front of me and shoved it toward him, repeating "*sawa-sawa—sawa-sawa.*" As I got lower he methodically lowered the crossbow, still pointing it at my chest. He had no expression. I watched his finger on the trigger; then we stared at each other.

Slowly I reached into my shirt pocket and groped for anything I could find. There was loose change and a Ugandan ten-shilling note, (worth about $1.50). I gradually pulled out the note and put it on the ground beyond the camera.

Nothing happened. We watched each other. I realized, to my added horror, that his arrow was tipped in resin which meant a poison of some kind. If I were shot, even slightly wounded, I would probably not survive.

After what seemed like an eternity he warily edged forward and picked up the money. He still held the crossbow with one hand. It was still cocked, still pointed at my chest. He backed away, lowered the weapon and unloaded the arrow. There were no sounds. Everything seemed to be in slow motion.

I picked up the camera, forced it into my backpack and stood up, then moved sideways, like a crab, worried that he would reload and shoot me in the back. I glanced up the road, to look where I was going, and when I turned back he had disappeared down the trail next to the road.

"Costly picture," I said half aloud. "I wonder if it is in focus."

I hiked—actually jogged—looking back several times until a truck came laboring through the hills. The front seat was full of market women, but the driver stopped and motioned me to the back. As

I watched his finger on the trigger, then we stared at each other.

A Bantu bird hunter with a traditional crossbow near Kabale, Uganda. (Author's collection)

I tossed my pack up and climbed in, a small boy of about nine years old greeted me with a huge smile. He began repeating "*Jambo, bwana, jambo, bwana.* (Hello, sir)." We shook hands.

"What a contrast you are," I said. "What a pleasant contrast!"

He didn't understand, but kept smiling and saying "*Jambo, bwana.*" After a while he got tired of talking, lay down on a pile of dry sacks and went to sleep.

Near the Uganda-Congo border at Kisoro was a place called Travelers Rest. It was in a lush rainforest, a remote safari camp and research station owned by a man named Walter Baumgartel, a German settler in Uganda. I had heard about him in Kampala and understood he was a serious primate researcher, reclusive, and usually unwelcoming—not the sort to drop in on or ask for shelter. On the other hand, it was almost dark, the border could be closed, and even if it was open I didn't relish going into the Congo at night.

None of the reports of Baumgartel were true. When I first saw him in the twilight he was sitting on his veranda under a thatched roof, writing notes and talking intently with a small African in a green shirt and green beret. When I introduced myself he extended his hand and then motioned to his companion.

"This is Ruben—the best tracker in Africa. He just told me the old male gorilla has died, probably of dysentery. There will be competition, even fighting for his harem."

I nodded and then asked if I could pay for shelter and a meal and, if possible, see the gorillas.

"First class or last class?" Baumgartel said, eyeing my backpack.

"Last...minus one," I said.

"I see," he said. "OK, pay Ruben 30 shillings ($4.00) for a tracking trip and you can sleep here. Ruben needs money or his wives will run away." Ruben shrugged, as if he had heard the comment a hundred times.

Over supper I told Baumgartel of my encounter with the crossbow hunter.

"Where was it?" he asked.

I got my tattered map and pecked on the place.

"Ah...yes," he said. "It was a forested area, right, after Kabale? A lot of those people are still living by hunting birds and small animals. They would be very superstitious about pictures. The man probably thought your taking his picture would somehow capture his soul."

The German paused and looked at me. "You put him in the position of saving his own soul from being stolen. For him it was almost like taking his life. You scared him deeply."

"He scared me deeply," I said.

Baumgartel thought for a while. "You did the right thing with the money...laying it on the road. Had he been drinking?"

I shrugged.

"Probably not," he said. "He would have shot you if he had. Most of the violence over there starts with the homemade *pombe* beer. Anyway, the man was Bantu, probably both a farmer and hunter. He would have deep beliefs in spirits and ancestors and a lot of ideas of what is evil in the world. He would believe it extremely dangerous to lose his spirit protectors. It would open him to all kinds of illness and danger, including endless bad luck in hunting."

"Did he see me as a witch?" I asked.

"Probably...yes," Baumgartel replied.

I shuddered and told him about William Hanning, the prospector killed in Gogoland, Tanganyika, I had read about on my first day in Africa. I suggested we had both been seen as *white* witches.

"Same thing, same exact thing," Baumgartel went on. "You both were perceived to be arch-enemies, totally evil. He was desecrating a gravesite, you were stealing a soul. Hanning lost. You survived."

There was a long silence.

"A lesson?" I asked.

"Maybe. Yes, I think so. Most uneducated Bantu believe deeply in witchcraft. Like medieval Europeans, witchcraft is part of the culture. The ideas let people blame someone else for bad luck, for death, injury, for anything. It's a tool. It is also believed an ordinary human can be a witch and keep it secret. Their power is unseen, hidden. It's a system based on fear and on using terror, blaming others, like scapegoats."

Baumgartel sensed my mood. "Look," he said. "You need a break from thinking about witchcraft. Go see the gorillas. Go with Ruben. He has another client for tomorrow. Get your mind off that stuff. It's a good hike. Very peaceful, my gorillas don't believe in witchcraft!"

Baumgartel laughed. "No one has ever been attacked. Bluff charges? Yes. Attacks? No. Don't worry."

Later that evening a mud-covered dark green Land Rover arrived and a Scottish physican named David Gillette strode onto the veranda. Yes, he would like a beer. Yes, he would like company tomorrow and no, I need not pay for gas. We spent the evening looking at local maps.

GORILLA ENCOUNTERS:
A DIVERSION FROM WITCHCRAFT

At dawn we picked up Ruben and drove through the lowlands, watching the distant Virunga mountains come into view through the morning mist, honking our way past laughing schoolchildren and a few old men with herds of goats. The land on both sides was tilled by women, many with babies strapped to their backs. A few laid down their hoes to wave or to toss their heads back to trill, and one old man stepped off the road, bowed and doffed his hat.

"Last vestige of our empire," Gillette said with a touch of nostalgia. "I think that old boy was from Congo—the Belgians still expect workers to bow."

With Ruben navigating, we drove into a lowland rainforest on increasingly slippery tracks, the Land Rover now constantly in four-wheel drive. After nearly an hour, round a bend, the track simply stopped in a clearing where a narrow path led up the mountain. Baumgartel had given us small day packs for cameras, water bottles and food but Ruben left his in the car, first wrapping his legs in green bands of cloth, then hanging a curved bush knife called a *rungu* on his belt.

When we headed up the trail the foliage closed in around us and the track started twisting over roots and jagged stones. Birds

"…my gorillas don't believe in witchcraft!"

called from both sides and within minutes sweat came through our shirts. The air was sultry and tiny hanging vines brushed my face. Gradually a canopy of trees closed tighter over our heads and the light faded. I felt a sense of foreboding. Small critters scurried in the underbrush and long black reptiles—almost certainly deadly snakes—turned out to be tree roots across the path.

In the first hour Gillette and I had trouble keeping up with Ruben who climbed with amazing agility, apparently assuming we were safe behind him. Finally, up ahead, he stopped and peered at the ground. Light brown dung lay on the track and Ruben touched it with the back of his knuckles, then whispered to Gillette.

"Cold, dry. Maybe yesterday, a *toto*. A young one." Gillette repeated.

...and for the first time that day I saw Ruben smile.

Ahead, near the trail, a clump of red flowers had been ripped up, half eaten and flung on the ground. To the right branches lay freshly trampled, some oozing white sap. Ruben picked up the flowers and again whispered to Gillette.

"They are called 'red hot pokers'," he said. "Gorillas will eat a fistful, then trample the rest. Strange behavior—maybe they are like hot peppers."

In a hundred yards the path leveled and then opened into a clearing where the foliage fell back, letting in slanting rays of sun. Long black vines with cracked bark hung from the trees, and across the clearing we came onto new signs. Moist dung shone in the mid-day sun. A shrub was pulled up, stripped of its leaves and tossed aside and small flat stones had been overturned for insects or grub worms. As we hiked further, the bush closed over our heads. In a few hundred feet Ruben pointed again and whispered to Gillette. The doctor nodded.

"A family of four or five were here this morning. That's the nest they built last night."

In a low thicket of bushes the gorillas had smashed down a round sleeping area some five feet across, and lined it with leaves. Dung droppings were around the edge and partially chewed leaves were scattered inside. We looked at each other, and for the first time that day I saw Ruben smile.

Ten minutes later we came over a ridge into another clearing where we could see off the trail. Ruben stopped, his head cocked sideways.

Suddenly from across the clearing there was a scream, then a bark and the head and shoulders of a gorilla appeared, then vanished. Nearby, monkey shrieks and loud bird cries erupted. As if in reply to the bark, several other barks came from further along the trail. For a split-second we saw the back of a smaller gorilla crashing deeper into the bush.

Ruben started to talk, but then twenty yards further up, near the clearing, a third, much bigger gorilla crashed out of the thicket and stood in the middle of the trail. As we watched it hunched forward and dug its fists into the ground, its deep-set eyes glowering at us. Then, with one bound it disappeared, following the others to the right. New sounds were everywhere, birdcalls, monkey howls, barks from at least two gorillas and as we listened, at least a dozen birds flew over our heads and into the trees. We moved ahead to the center of the opening, near a sharply eroded cliff.

A minute later, off the trail from where we had come, another bark pierced the air. Ruben raised his arm and made a half circle suggesting at least one gorilla had gotten behind us, near the trail that led down the mountain. That reality made me uneasy but both Ruben and the doctor looked totally relaxed. Gillette was smiling and seemed to think we had seen the last of the gorillas. He held up three fingers as a sign of triumph and reached for a cigarette. He was fumbling for his lighter when a fourth animal broke. He dropped the cigarette.

This animal was huge, almost certainly the one trying to take over the harem. It simply glared at us. Then the impossible happened. It charged! It came straight at us running with fantastic speed, first on its hind legs then lunging forward to catch balance, then moving on all fours. It came twenty-five yards across

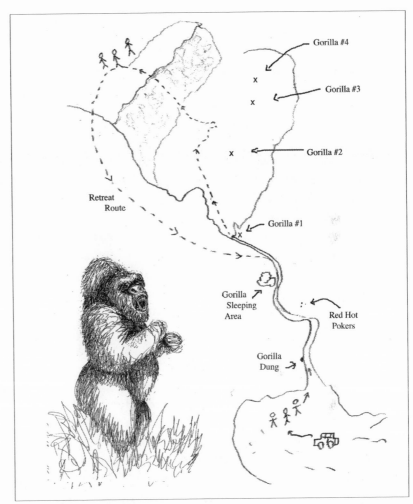

Gorilla #4

Gorilla #3

Gorilla #2

Gorilla #1

Retreat
Route

Gorilla
Sleeping
Area

Red Hot
Pokers

Gorilla
Dung

The author's sketch map and drawing from his trek to observe lowland mountain gorillas in the Virunga mountains of the Uganda–Congo borderlands. (Redrawn by Eden Abram)

the clearing, then stopped. Its shoulders were twice as broad as a man's, its huge head twitched from side to side, and its black eyes glared at us.

Ruben looked stricken, his eyes wide, his mouth open. This was our tracker, this was the man who had been so calm facing other gorillas. Now everything was different. He jabbered to Gillette, who paled, then translated in short breaths.

"First stage of a charge…could attack any minute…. It is the one who took over the females…Ruben has never seen it so angry."

I began to feel sick. My throat was parched. I got dizzy. I seemed to be disoriented. Our way to the immediate left was blocked by a tangle of vines. The gorilla was straight ahead. To our right, back down the trail, was possible if the other animal would not harm us. It was our only way out because behind us was the steep escarpment, a sheer cliff with jagged stones and protruding washed-out roots. We started to move down the trail as the big male watched, his head jerking from side to side.

"Try to look small, don't make eye contact," Gillette said.

This time the gorilla seemed to be catapulted from where he stood. He came straight across the clearing and cut off our escape. He stood, screamed and pounded his chest. We were trapped!

Every detail of the animal was magnified. His nostrils moved slowly in and out. His chest heaved. Big white teeth were exposed through the curled lips. Then slowly he settled into a crouch, the hair on his neck sticking straight up. Tiny beady eyes smoldered as he turned his head back and forth as he hunched forward, his knuckles digging into the ground, the fingers turned up, flexing. Then he charged again!

He shot towards us, slowed, stopped, stood up, pounded his chest, then side-stepped into a thicket of bushes, still glaring at us.

Ruben spat words. Gillette's eyes widened.

"He's going to attack!"

As I watched him, Ruben motioned to the escarpment, the

cliff behind us. It looked impossible. We ran to the base, spread out and started clawing our way up, grabbing at roots. Dirt and small stones rolled down the slope. My fingers began to bleed, the knees of my pants tore, my legs ached. I was sure the gorilla was behind me. It was the kind of terrifying dream I remembered as a kid.

Nobody looked back. Gillette was coughing and wheezing as he climbed. Ruben on the other hand was already above us, scrambling up with amazing agility.

"Some damn guide, you are," I said half aloud. "You are supposed to protect us."

Then, from above, Ruben turned and listened. I stopped climbing, held onto a root and looked down. There was nothing there. No sound, no lunging gorilla, just the wind whistling through the grass from below. In a moment Ruben climbed over the edge and pulled Gillette up. I waved him off, grabbed a clump of grass and crawled over. We all knelt, the doctor groping for a cigarette, then trying to light it as his hands shook. No one spoke.

In a few minutes Ruben nodded and we followed him down the back slope. When we were below where the gorillas might be, we cut a path back to the main trail and hurried to the Land Rover, stowed the gear and rumbled into the lowlands. Nobody talked. At the lodge Baumgartel greeted us warmly, shrugged off the confrontation and asked detailed questions about the condition of the four gorillas. He seemed pleased they looked healthy.*

That night, over dinner, when we had exhausted the gorilla stories, I asked Dr. Gillette about his experiences with witchcraft beliefs among his patients. He had been in Uganda eight years and had worked in both local clinics and at the national hospital.

"Sure," he said, "big topic for any western trained doctor around here...because we don't understand much about African traditional medicine. Witchcraft beliefs are apart of that system, traditional healers use it as a diagnosis, an explanation for a lot of tragedy and illness and most people see a traditional healer before they get to a clinic...hell, there are thousands of these healers across Uganda, millions in Africa. They all use witchcraft as a reason for illness."

He paused to let the German comment, but Baumgartel nodded his agreement.

"Look, a lot of these healers do good work, they are needed, counselors, good citizens. Remember we are talking about a whole range of people...herbalists, root collectors, midwives, general healers, people who do minor surgery, dentistry, counselors like psychiatrists in the west. The big problem...two problems actually.

"First, as I said, they use witchcraft as a diagnosis and thus perpetuate the beliefs which are bogus...nonesense... its malaria that killed the baby, not the "witch" next door. The other big issues is that the traditional healers are prescribing all kinds of medicines that we in clinic don't know anything about. How in the hell can I treat a very ill patient that can't tell me what's in his stomach...what's working on him, on his blood chemistry. Even if we get the local name of a medicine, how do we know what it's properties are. Big problem...where African and the west come to crunch...in the guy's stomach."

The next morning as I got ready to hike out of Baumgartel's camp toward the Congo border, I again offered to pay for the lodging, but the German dismissed me with a wave of his hand.

"You earned it. You are a good reporter. You told me my gorillas are healthy, dats good."

He smiled faintly and then handed me a note.

"On the other side," he said, "go find Jean Pierre Hallet. Give him this note. Tell him you are a friend of mine. Ask him about your witchcraft business among the pygmies... he knows a lot."

When I was there in 1960, just across the Uganda–

Jean Pierre Hallet, Goma, Belgian Congo, 1960.

A Pygmy boy on a vine

Congo border, in the area around Goma was a region of spectacular beauty. Lakes nestled between small vine-covered mountains and small volcanoes belched tiny puffs of smoke. Hundreds of streams came rushing off the slopes, and there were carpets of flowers along the roadside, a constant fragrance in the cool air.

At that time, the Batwa (Pygmies) lived just to the north in the Ituri forest. In the town I first came to, Goma, they had a patron, Jean Pierre Hallet, a Belgian who had lost one hand dynamiting fish on one of the lakes. He had studied the Batwa and for several years collected Congolese art for his trading post, a place that looked like an open-air museum. Hallet studied the note from Baumgartel with pursed lips and a wide-eyed, playful stone face.

"Ah, the old German with the great apes," he exclaimed. "How is he? How is old Baumgartel? How are the apes? I love the apes."

Before I could answer, he clapped me on the shoulder.

"Let's go. I was just going up to the forest to collect things, plenty of things." He then stopped and looked me up and down. "You eat monkey meat, no? All Americans eat monkey meat. I know this. There was one here a year ago! An American, not a monkey."

After an hour of driving over dirt roads, then tracks and then wide trails, he parked the truck in a clearing and sat in silence. In about ten minutes a Batwa carrying a bow and a quiver of arrows appeared from the bush, greeted us and put his bow and quiver on the ground. Hallet gave him a packet of sugar and a packet of tea, locked the car, and handed the man the keys.

"He is my guard," Hallet said. "The keys give him great authority. They are our bond. I trust him, he trusts me. Let's go. The trail is there."

Within two miles, we came onto the edge of a clearing. A child swung on a low vine and several women prepared food in huts near the edge of the forest. Smoke from several fires circled into the trees.

In the village, Hallet was greeted with hand claps and whistling, laughter and a lot of merriment. He obviously loved being here and began jabbering to the leader in a combination of French and Swahili. A child brought the Batwa man a straw hat, which apparently marked his rank when visitors were about.

"Do you have any cigarettes?" Hallet asked. "They want to shoot cigarettes off a stick. They like to show their marksmanship."

"I don't smoke," I said.

"OK," said Hallet. "Give them any small change you have. They can use that too."

I dug out several East African shillings the size of American quarters. The Batwa leader found some sticks, slit the ends and slipped the coins into the slots, then stuck the sticks into the ground across the clearing.

Several of the men lined up, still laughing and joking with each other. With a nod from an elder, they started shooting. The coins went down immediately. Children rushed out to set up the sticks and the process was repeated. In a few minutes Hallet waved for them to stop. He walked out and with great fanfare, turned the sticks sideways so that the target was the thin edge of the coin.

There were four coins on four sticks about 25 yards away. A few of the children shot first and all missed. Then four of the senior hunters stepped up, and on some silent signal simultaneously shot all four coins into the air. It was amazing marksmanship. Hallet tried a few shots and

A. Pygmy shooters

B. Author shooting at big leaves

C. Individual shooting

*D. Pygmy family.
(Author's collection)*

*A marksmanship demonstration in a Batwa village in the Ituri forest, near Bunia, in the Belgian Congo involving a group of hunters, an individual marksman with a cigarette, the author and his instructor and the instructor's family.
(Author's collection, 1960)*

missed. He gave me the bow and a few arrows, and all three shots went into the ground. Everyone laughed and pointed at the ground. As the crowd dispersed, one of the elders spoke to Hallet.

"He says you shoot like a child...and you should take a lesson from one of them."

"Fine, fine, let's do it," I said.

My teacher was the boy who had been swinging on the vines. He patiently stuck big leaves into the ends of the stick, and began the lesson. Shot after shot I hit nothing. Finally, to my relief, a woman called from across the clearing. My teacher shrugged and beckoned for me to follow. His mother and father were seated by a fire. This time, with permission assured by Hallet, I was able to get a family portrait, including my teacher and his bow.

The group of Batwa I visited, were as Audrey Richards suggested, a study in human adaptability. Jean Pierre Hallet said they were not really nomadic, but "transhumant," moving just a few times a year. He reported they divided their territory into quadrants and migrated

A collection of Batwa hunting arrows from the Ituri forest, Eastern Congo: A. Metal penetrating arrow for small animals, B. Long distance wooden penetrating arrow, C. Blunt wooden arrow for killing with high impact, D. Metal penetrating arrow, E. Metal arrow with poison grooves. Lower left, Batwa leather quiver with arrows on antelope skin. (Author's collection)

Batwa village chief with grandson. (Author's collection)

periodically from one to another to conserve the plants and animals. This group survived by gathering edible plants and hunting monkeys, antelopes and rodents. At very specific times in the plant cycle they obtained their medicines from forest roots and plants.

Bumping back to Goma, Hallet and I talked about Batwa Pygmy religion and witchcraft. They believed in both a forest god and a high god or creator. Like the Sandawe I had met earlier in Kondoa and like most hunter-gatherers, including the San (Bushmen) in Botswana and South Africa, they did not embrace witchcraft unless they settled near African Bantu farmers. Then, even for a short period of time, they adopted witchcraft beliefs and bought amulets and medicines for protection. When they went back to their traditional lifestyle, they dropped the beliefs. As hunter-gatherers, Pygmies did not need witchcraft. The information lent credibility to the theory that Stone Age people did not embrace witchcraft until they settled, cultivated, and developed larger, more complex societies.

Later I asked Hallet how the Batwa settled disputes, if they used witchcraft accusations or threats of witchcraft to force people out of their villages. The Belgian looked at me and shook his head, as if it were common knowledge and I was the only one in the dark.

"They don't use witchcraft...they settle disputes like their ancestors did," he said. "They shoot each other in the back with poisoned arrows." He turned the palm of his one good hand up and frowned in mock sadness. "Poor Ndugu," he said. "He stepped right in front of my arrow as I shot at the monkey...the bush was so thick. Poor Ndugu."

Before we parted, Hallet presented me with a quiver of Batwa arrows with the poison supposedly boiled off the tips. "But just in case it is not all gone, don't stick your finger with one of these." He then said something I would remember for a long time. "Even the idea of poison does funny things to people who believe in witchcraft."

Over the next two weeks, I trekked back into Uganda, to Murchison Falls National Park on the Nile, and spent a week camping, birdwatching and game-watching. The falls themselves were spectacular, the river at this point crashing through a twenty-eight foot ravine into pools of crocodile-infested backwaters. It was here I first heard of the relationship between witchcraft and poison made from crocodile bile.

Eric van der Whipple was a hunter of Dutch ancestry who lived outside Murchison Park in a rambling thatched-roof house overlooking the Nile. He made his living as a guide for European hunting par-

Eric van der Whipple, a Dutch national who worked near Murchison Falls on the Nile as a crocodile hunter, hide merchant and hunting guide. (Author's collection)

ties, and in his spare time shot crocodiles along the river for their meat and hides. He described himself as a hunter and hide merchant, and claimed to have three wives, all Ugandan princesses. I only met one, a gracious, beautiful lady named Constance, and their three children. Later Constance quietly told me he only dreamed of three wives.

Van der Whipple was able to explain something about poison made from crocodile bile. The liver and bile of a crocodile are traditionally believed to be so poisonous that African crocodile hunters, particularly on the shores of Lake Victoria, must be seen to cut out the organs and burn them or throw them into the water, lest they be accused of manufacturing poison for sale to those who practice witchcraft.

"Does the poison work?" I asked.

He shrugged. "I hear the fisheries officers on Lake Victoria have sent some croc liver and bile to London for a lab test. It came back negative, 'non toxic.' But," he went on, "when they told this to an old fisherman, he said to wait until he could bring in other ingredients. He came with the powdered roots of two plants. Again they sent the powders off to London with the croc bile, and this time it came back toxic—really toxic. Apparently the roots combine with the liver and bile to cause a chemical change. It is beyond me but that's what I understand."

"And the witchcraft connection?" I asked, thinking of Jean Pierre Hallet in the Congo and his suggestion that the *idea* of poison can do strange things to people's minds.

"I see witchcraft around here as two kinds," Eric said. "First there is the 'scare them with words' form of witchcraft, people intimidating each other with imaginary terror reports, like their ability to control a wild beast, the impossible claims. Then there is the real thing, when poisons are used to kill someone, for revenge or money, and it is blamed on *uchawi*. Witchcraft is the cover-up, the camouflage."

He fell silent for a moment.

"I can get you a packet, a little packet of dried poison. You can put it with your Pygmy arrows and let an American lab test it for you."

"Thanks," I said. "I'm going to have enough trouble getting my arrows through customs. I have the Sudan border to get across, plus a lot of others."

At Nimule, on the Uganda–Sudan border, I was detained by a very tall, very polite Sudanese immigration officer. He thought it was a bad idea that I start walking north from his border post and insisted I wait for a long-distance truck going to Juba.

"Why would the driver take me?" I asked, watching another tall Sudanese clean his rifle. The immigration officer yawned, took off his khaki field hat and adjusted the black feather in the brim.

"Because I will tell him to take you. And, you will give him cigarettes."

Something told me it was going to be a long wait. That afternoon I bought food from the little market down the hill, and that night slept in the guardhouse storeroom. The next day I sat in the shade of a mango tree and wrote field notes, trying to recall the lessons learned across East Africa, particularly about witchcraft.

In truth, I had not gotten very far into African culture. I had learned only "baby" Swahili and, with a few exceptions, had drifted from one European enclave to another, benefiting from the privileged treatment white people got in colonial Africa. True, I had stayed overnight in African homes, but my hosts were relatively affluent truck drivers, teachers or storekeepers who lived in a basic western lifestyle. I had not witnessed a witchcraft incident, nor watched a witchcraft case unfold in the courts. I did learn the hard way that anyone can be taken for a witch, including Europeans, including William Hanning and myself.

I discovered that most of the stereotypes about Africa and Africans were just wrong. The western media still portrayed Africa with deep jungles, and Africans as savages with skins and beads or as loyal gun-bearers to fearless white hunters. I met no one, aside from the man with the crossbow, who qualified as dangerous in any way. People were curious and inviting, open, friendly and far less hidebound by religion than I had encountered in India. On the road I found I could ask anyone for help and anyone for shelter.

In those days the Sudanese and Ugandan border posts were close to each other and officials strolled easily between the buildings, trading cigarettes and talking endlessly about the young women in the market.

The men all spoke some English. Three were Muslim, two Christian, and three were what one of the Ugandans called "pagan boys." After a day and a half, I felt comfortable enough to ask about their beliefs.

The eight men gave me one final lesson in witchcraft. All said they believed firmly in it, but none had any problem holding the ideas in tandem with their religious faiths. This was understandable for the "pagan boys," but the doctrines of both Christianity and Islam strongly deny the existence of witchcraft. Somewhere I had seen this situation referred to as a "duality of mind," the ability to simultaneously hold two conflicting ideas. I did not know it at the time, but this mixing and meshing of ideas was going to cause me a lot of trouble in understanding witchcraft.

The next day, just before I was put on a mud-splattered truck with 200 reeking cowhides going to a tannery in Juba, I had an epiphany. I would come back to East Africa. I would study Swahili and live in a village. I would learn what it was like to live with witches. I would try to see witchcraft through African eyes.

2

Living with Witches

1964-1966

Kabota Sadoka, translator, Tabora, Tanzania
Chief John Mtura Mdeka, Usagari village, Tanzania
Mohammadi Lupanda, woman accused of witchcraft
Mabubu Mahezya, leader in a witchcraft trial
Ian Harker, Australian forester, Tabora, Tanzania
Peter Rigby, anthropologist, Dodoma, Tanzania
Juma Kabena, retired government messenger, Ibiri, Tanzania

Nearly four years after my first trek across East Africa, I returned to Kenya, this time not on a freighter from India but on an aging VC10 jet from London. While I was away, between 1960 and 1964, all three East African countries had gained independence and all three encountered serious problems with witchcraft. Tanganyika's new government, under Julius Nyerere, immediately confronted a series of murders in witchcraft "covens" along the Rufiji River that made headlines for months. Uganda's President Milton Obote faced a series of vigilante killings of alleged witches

* My return to the region was thanks to new American interest in Africa and the availability of study grants. I had passed through a graduate program in African politics and anthropology, studied Swahili and received funding for two years of field research for a doctoral thesis. The topic was the grass-roots political and economic changes that had occurred after independence in Kenya and Tanzania. (Tanganyika became the United Republic of Tanzania in 1964 with the merger of the mainland and Zanzibar).

in his first year, many near the Congo border. In President Jomo Kenyatta's Kenya, the new Parliament debated the merits of forming a "national witchcraft commission," particularly to counter the violence on their coast. *

Because of the unrest, each government launched campaigns against witchcraft, mainly through large public meetings, with endless harangues by African officials that people should give up witchcraft and stop "primitive practices.'" In Kenya public confessions were encouraged as well as the burning of suspected witchcraft paraphernalia, although many of the items were for traditional healing. It was the same confusion between healing and witchcraft practices that Walter Reece had pointed out on my first trip.

In Nairobi I bought a tent, a lot of other camping gear, tools, and an aged Land Rover that the African mechanic called "*mzee*" (old man). I decided to keep the name, and well before dawn three days later Mzee and I left Nairobi for Arusha, Tanzania, stayed overnight in a Peace Corps hostel, and then pressed south. I camped with Hamisi Ali and his goats near Cheke III and again heard of his hopes for a second wife. The next day, a flat tire and a broken water hose later, I came into the outskirts of Tabora, the regional capital and market center of around 10,000 people. It was a low-slung and dusty place.

Tabora had been an Arab slave-collecting point in the 18th and 19th centuries, and after 1885 a German administrative post. Here, at the center of their sprawling colony, then called Tanganyika, the Germans built a railway junction, a large white fort with ramparts and, curiously, a small opera house.

My first step was to present my Tanzanian research clearance to the new African District Commissioner, a man named John Kamata. The clearance had been issued by the central government, but I had to have district-level approval to proceed. Fieldwork is at once the raw material of all social science research and it was crucial that I get past this barrier.

As Kamata studied the letter, I worried that there might be a lot of explaining to do. He looked serious as he put down the paper and took off his glasses.

"Good. Welcome! Very important work," he said with a sudden

Kenya government programs to stamp out witchcraft included orchestrated public confessions, the handing out of pamphlets explaining the illegality of witchcraft and the burning of confiscated items (which included calabashes, horns, shells, bones, animal teeth, gourds and carrying bags) in Eldoret, Kenya, 1965. Kenya District Officer in the background (wearing helmet). (Kenya Ministry of Information)

A. Village scenes from Usagari, Tanzania include the road from Tabora to Usagari.

smile. "We need people in America to understand Africa. We are glad to have you." As I breathed a sigh of relief he tapped his pencil on the letter and gazed out the window. "Now, where do you want to work? What village? What about a translator into the local Nyamwezi language, a research assistant? Maybe I can help."

Within three days I had found an assistant, located a village, met the local headman and been offered a room in an old, abandoned chief's compound. Later I learned that Kabota Sadoka, my new translator, was the District Commissioner's nephew and secretly reported our activities to him at least once a week.

The village, called Usagari, was 24 miles northwest of Tabora and had a population of just over 600. There was a *duka* (store) run by an Arab family from Oman, a primary school, a tiny infirmary, two tea houses and an unused political party office. At the entrance to the village, a collection of lion skulls on a bush were warnings to both lions and witches to stay away from the village.

B. Lion skulls on a bush near the village entrance.
C. The general store with Omani store keepers.
D. Local chief, John Mtura Mdeka with his senior wife in ceremonial regalia, near his ritual hut.
E. Translator Kabota Sadoka with his friend and child near the author's compound.
(Author's collection)

In fact, Usagari was the name of both the village and the surrounding chiefdom, an area of about eighty square miles. Outside the village center most of the population lived in dispersed homesteads, their compounds intermingled with fields of maize, beans and cassava. Since the 1750s, Arab slavers had crisscrossed this area, converting the Nyamwezi to a watered-down version of Islam and, from Tabora town, launching caravans to the coast with slaves carrying ivory. Nineteenth-century explorers David Livingston, Henry Morton Stanley, Richard Burton, John Speke and John Grant had each passed through here in search of the source of the Nile, or in the case of Stanley, in search of David Livingston.

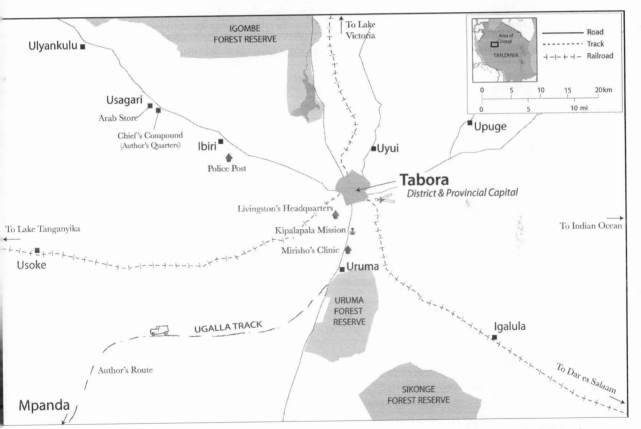

Tabora Region, Central Tanzania, including Usagari and other villages in which the author worked. (Map by Ellen Kozak)

The land around Usagari was a rolling savannah called *miombo* bush, named for the short scrub trees that flourished in the dry soils. Both German and British colonials had used the traditional chiefs to govern in an "indirect rule" system, and Usagari was one of six chiefdoms spread out on the Tabora-Ulyankulu road.

In Ulyankulu village, the road simply stopped. To the west, toward the Congo, lay 300 miles of desolation. Because of sleeping sickness from the tsetse fly most of that region was uninhabited except for an untold number of gazelles, sable, wild pig, hyena, lion and elephant.

The ex-chief of Usagari, John Mtura Mdeka, was technically out of power because the new government had appointed village administrators. Nobody paid any attention to that decree, however, and the administrator never came to Usagari. Mdeka was a convivial man in his late forties, a farmer, with a homestead a mile from the old chief's compound where I had been given a room.

The compound was on a hill, a one-story, U-shaped structure. Much of the building's cement was crumbling, and the thatch over several rooms was open to the sky. My room, however, was freshly painted, the thatch repaired and the cement floor scrubbed. Hot water was heated over an open fire in the back courtyard and beyond was a walled-off pit latrine and "bathhouse" with a tiny stool and ladle to splash water from a big pot. To move in I only needed a cot, a canvas chair, a camp table and a kerosene lamp.

Kabota, my assistant, found lodging in the village center with "cousins," which meant he had located a remote kinship tie and was paying token rent. One of his "cousins," a woman in her late thirties with a daughter, agreed to provide meals for us and bring firewood and water. She smiled a lot at Kabota and later I learned she was not his cousin at all but his private cook and bed partner.

Five weeks after we arrived in Usagari, a public witchcraft accusation was leveled against a widow living behind us near the edge of the village. The situation was serious and a group of elders was convened.

Accused witch Mohammadi Lupanda, Usagari village, with neighbor children, and enroute from well carrying firewood. (Author's collection)

With difficulty Kabota managed to gain permission from the elders for us to observe, mainly I suspect because the meeting was held near the old headquarters where I slept.

Mohammadi Lupanda, age 52, who lived alone a quarter mile from her bachelor brother, was accused of witchcraft by two neighbors. She was found near their houses late at night, wailing and making strange sounds. Two days later a four-week-old baby girl died, and the accusation of killing a child by witchcraft was made against her.

I had met Mohammadi several times as she came by my compound from the nearby well. She always greeted me with a curtsey and a soft "*Jambo, bwana*" (hello, sir). She was a small woman with somber brown eyes, her hair neatly braided. I knew she had a pair of red flip-flops, but when she carried water she was always barefoot, probably so as not to slip where water had been splashed. Most women balanced their water buckets on their heads but Mohammadi carried the bucket on her hip and often dragged sticks of firewood behind her. When I interviewed her brother, a village farmer, Mohammadi sat with us, preparing cassava roots and tossing the peelings to her chickens. She did not speak up often, although she did gently correct her brother on many of his answers.

Because the accusation was serious, the elders sent for a man who had been a sub-chief under the colonial system. Since independence he had switched jobs to become an organizer in a political party then called the Tanzania African National Union, (TANU). In fact, the gathering was illegal from the point of view of the government, as well as the national party, a detail that didn't concern the elders or the leader, Mabubu Mahezya.

The group met in the late afternoon under a spreading mango tree, all sitting on small stools, a few women watching and listening nearby while they hoed. After the allegations by the two family heads, the leader Mahezya turned to Mohammadi and asked her to speak. She sat next to her brother, her hair freshly combed and braided, her shoulders wrapped in an orange shawl called a *kikoi*. Her first words were barely audible, and the group simultaneously leaned forward to hear her.

"I'm not *mchawi* (a witch)," she said. "I do not practice *uchawi*. I am sometimes sick, and when I carry my water from the well at sunset, I call out only to scare the wild pigs away and to let people know I am passing."

Her brother nodded as she spoke.

"I came from Ibiri seven years ago," she continued. "I cook for my brother and live in a separate house and tend our fields. I am poor. I have no animals, only four chickens, two black, two orange." A cloud came over her face and she stopped talking. I thought she might cry, but then she composed herself. "I left Ibiri because my only child, a two-year-old girl, died eight years ago. I never quarrel with my neighbors. I am a good person. I am not evil."

One of the aggrieved men contradicted her. He said she had been driven out of Ibiri village as a witch and that since she had come to

Usagari both she and her brother had been hoarding land and not allowing anyone else to use it, even after it had lain fallow for two seasons. Another man murmured she was "*mbaya* (bad)." The father of the dead child did not speak, but stared at Mohammadi.

When everyone had spoken, the leader said he would investigate the allegations in Ibiri. He ended the meeting with an invocation to keep the peace in the name of TANU, and the President, *Mwalimu* (teacher) Julius Nyerere. He motioned to a child to bring his bicycle, climbed onto it, and slowly pedaled up the road toward Ulyankulu.

Before that investigation occurred, a second report circulated that Mohammadi had been seen yet again, wailing at night, near the same neighbor's house, this time naked. Another meeting was hurriedly called.

This gathering was larger and the atmosphere tense. Greetings were muted, and most people sat quietly on small stools brought by children. When the official arrived he was dusty and sweating and openly annoyed at having had to ride so far, so soon. He conferred briefly with

The healer and diviner, Hamisi Juma, with his assistant, Jamal, in Usagari village, Tanzania. (Author's collection)

four of the elders, then sent a boy in a green TANU Youth League shirt to bring Mohammadi, and to find Hamisi Juma, a healer.

While we waited I asked Kabota about the healer. He was known to be a member of a spirit medium cult, the Baswezi, and believed able to control spirits and to serve as a go-between for an ill person and the spirit world. He was also said to be able to identify witches. Jamal, his assistant, who looked to be on *bhang* (hemp) most of the time, prepared medicines and drummed for Juma in healing ceremonies.

The second meeting was opened by the leader with a clap of his hands. He asked for discussion, and one man after another argued that Mohammadi must be banished. One elder stated he was afraid of her, another said she would ruin the crops or spoil their wives' pregnancies. A bald old man suggested she did not use precious land and should be beaten. No one suggested she was sick or possibly mentally ill.

Hamisi Juma, the diviner, was asked to speak, and in a high-pitched, squeaky voice repeated what had already been said. He then stood up and offered to conduct a witch-hunting ceremony if 200 shillings could be collected from all the villagers. No one was interested and the leader Mahezya motioned him to sit down.

Mohammadi was then told to speak and all eyes turned to watch her. First she told of her child's death and that at times she believed the child was not really dead, but only lost. Sometimes she dreamed the child was calling her and, because she is a mother, she would go out in the night to look for her. Mohammadi said that had been the case when the neighbors found her wandering near their homes, but that she was not naked.

"I cry out for my lost child," she said. "Yes, I stood out there that night, but near my doorway. I must bring my child home. I am sick and have only cassava to eat."

Again she denied doing things that brought witchcraft, but this time she began ticking items off on her fingers. "I do not send insects against people," she said. "I do not beat figures drawn on the ground with branches, nor put poisoned thorns near a person's hut where they go to urinate. I don't buy bad *dawa* (medicine) in the market. I don't put it in people's beer pots."

> *"I do not bring* fisi *or* simba *(hyena, lion) to the village. I am not a mchawi,"* she concluded.

Her voice was trembling. She paused and looked at the leader. There was fear in her eyes. "I do not bring *fisi* or *simba* (hyena, lion) to the village. I am not a *mchawi*," she concluded.

The group was silent. Then the diviner, Hamisi Juma, motioned that he would like to speak. He stood again, cleared his throat and looked straight at Mohammadi. His eyes were piercing and his head bobbed slowly. In his high-pitched, squeaky voice he said just one sentence. "She knows the methods very well."

The meeting exploded in angry voices. Some called for her banishment that day. The bald old man again suggested a beating, another pronounced her evil, and yet another claimed she had caused two other deaths. An elder who stuttered cursed her, spittle spraying from his mouth. A man in the back said that the pair of hyenas seen a month ago were probably under her control. Someone referred to the red shawl as a color witches like, and said he had smelled smoke and rotten meat late that night near her house, both signs of witchcraft.

There was a lull, and then a bookish young man with Coke-bottle glasses named Saidi Ulanga explained that the insects that Mohammadi referred to could have carried illness and killed the baby, and that she could have controlled the insects.

Finally, Mahezya the leader from Ulyankulu clapped for silence and then spoke, not looking at Mohammadi. "She must be a *mchawi*," he said. "Everyone believes this. She must be sent away. She must go. That is the wish of the people. That is our judgment."

Mahezya said he would send her back to Ibiri to live near the police post where she could be watched. He then looked directly at Mohammadi. "Be ready tomorrow, for the afternoon bus. Youth League boys will carry your parcels. You cannot stay."

Mohammadi looked at him and then stared at the ground, shaking her head and repeating that she was sick and would starve. Nobody listened. Nobody spoke to her. Most men got up and pushed their stools to children who had been summoned. Three of the elders gathered in a group, but most walked away. The women who had been hoeing huddled together, watching Mohammadi. None came forward.

The next day I watched from a distance as Mohammadi was led to the bus. Again no one spoke to her or helped her, except a boy who climbed to the top of the bus to tie down her three parcels. When the engine started and black diesel smoke belched into the road, several people began to jeer. One man spat at the bus. Someone else shouted "*mchawi* (witch)," and another repeated it. As the bus lurched forward in the ruts, I could see Mohammadi holding tightly to the seat in front of her. She kept looking back, watching the group. She had no expression. I wanted to wave, but for some reason couldn't raise my arm. I just watched as the bus belched diesel smoke, rocked in the ruts, then finally disappeared over Unga hill.

During Mohammadi's trial I noticed Kabota repeatedly looking at one of the women hoeing nearby. She was about his age, wrapped in a blue and white *kikoi* and working with a *jembe,* the wide-bladed hoe. A few days after Mohammadi's departure, in the village tea shop, I asked him about her.

"Kabota, the woman in the blue and white *kikoi?* You seem to know her?"

He hesitated, then leaned forward. "She was involved in another witchcraft case here in Usagari, about seven years ago. An old chief was poisoned...she went to jail for it. The police put her in jail."

"Another witchcraft case!" I exclaimed. "Why didn't you tell me? How did you know this? You are not from here!"

Kabota looked pained. He shifted in his seat, then leaned even closer and spoke in a low voice. "I was in jail too. In the Tabora prison. Then we called it the King's *hoteli.* The women's prison was close. We all knew the women. We saw them on work details. We knew her story."

He acted embarrassed, then looked at the ground. "I was only in jail five months," he said.

I fought the urge to ask *why* he was in jail at all. Kabota sensed the question and kept the conversation going on the woman. "We can see the records of her trial...they are public, at the court in Tabora."

A week later, after an old clerk slowly hand-copied my research

"I was only in jail five months."

clearance for his records, I was ushered to a small table and given a file tied with green twine. Across it was stamped "Case Closed." I untied the packet and began to read.

The record showed that the 82-year-old chief Mdeka of Usagari had died soon after the youngest of his four wives—the woman Kabota knew—put a red powder in his evening beer pot. He died near midnight after some shouting and other noises. Because of the commotion a constable was called and soon the police were involved. Under questioning, the young wife, Welelo Mkombe, admitted the act.

Curiously, two weeks later the red powder found near the chief's body—which had been sent to the government laboratory in Dar es Salaam for analysis—was determined to be non-toxic and harmless. Because of her confession Welelo was brought to trial only for *attempted murder*, found guilty, and sentenced to five years in prison.

For me, sitting there in the clerk's office, the trial record raised a lot of questions. What really killed the chief? It could have been a heart attack, or a convulsion brought on by rancid beer. Was there another poison involved, or other foul play? Poor forensic work by the government obscured the facts. Earlier, a Nyamwezi proverb I had read gave me a clue: "Wicked chiefs sometimes take 'hot food' (poison)." From three of my friends in Usagari village, the schoolteacher, the tea-house owner and one of the elders, I pieced together more of the story.

After her prison term, Welelo returned to Usagari and talked openly about her experiences. The teacher reported she claimed to have been encouraged by others in the village to administer the powder because many of the elders were tired of the local taxes and traditional tribute (a portion of any harvest or hunted meat was expected by the old chief). The schoolteacher said unrest in the face of the impending state independence hurt the chief's reputation. New political recruiters, the *kiongozis* or spearheads, were calling all chiefs lackeys of the colonial regime and there was agreement in the village for the chief's removal.

Another issue of interest was the poison. I recalled from Eric van der Whipple's lessons on crocodile bile that even harmless poisons can be a strong placebo and can cause enormous fear. Here the red pow-

Criminal Case JPCF 4, 26/7/58.

The Prisoner States:

"The son of the late Chief persuaded me to be his mistress from last year. His name was (deleted). I refused to be his mistress. He asked me why I refused when his father was an old man. In the end I agreed. I slept with him two nights just before Ramadan. After that he told me that he would look for a medicine to kill his father and that after his death he would be able to be my lover without fear. (Named) came to me at about 9.00 in the night of the death. At that time the deceased was in the verandah of the house before a fire with his three other children. (Named individual) returned to his house and came back to me again at 10:00 p.m. When he came I was taking water to the back yard. When the deceased went to take his bath (the named individual) came in and gave me the medicine and in his presence I put the poison in the liquor which was at the house.

"The poison was red and wrapped up in a piece of paper. He left immediately. The deceased came in after his bath and asked for the liquor. I gave him the native liquor in which the poison was placed.
"The deceased went to bed after drinking the liquor. I slept that night with the deceased. At 12 o'clock in the night the deceased started vomiting. Then he fell on the floor."

From the District Court Record, Tabora, Tanzania, 1965.
(Translated from the Nyamwezi by Court Clerk)

der may have been a placebo that terrified an 82-year-old man. He may have been frightened to death.

There was also the local explanation for the chief's death, after the government confirmed the powder was harmless. In fact, nobody cared about the government evidence. The consensus in the village was that Welelo used witchcraft, but then I learned that she had never been accused of witchcraft, either before or after the death. I was told she simply had witchcraft powers that night.

Later, Kabota reported that the color of the powder was important. As in the Mohammadi case, witchcraft is associated with red and black, and the red powder was seen as evidence of witchcraft. If she told the chief he had been poisoned, the young wife may have frightened him to death. Did she tell him about the poison before he died? That was the question. We needed to find an answer.

Two months later I reluctantly decided to put the Usagari cases aside and stick to my plan to do further research in southern Tanzania, in Rungwe District, among the coffee- and tea-growing people, the Nyakyusa. An Australian forester named Ian Harker, who worked on a foreign aid project in Tabora, offered to go with me so he could study the *miombo* woodlands south of Tabora, across miles of desolate bush country.

The problem was to find our way over 220 miles of dirt tracks, some through deep elephant grass, then to find a river crossing on the Ugalla River, ford the river, get fuel in Mpanda town and try not to break an axle and have to walk out through tsetse fly country. We studied early reports on the area and pored over the old German maps. The track we needed disappeared in several places on the best map we had, which meant we would have to drive by compass. We loaded extra food and fuel, a heavy axe and two shovels, a second spare tire, two head nets for tsetse flies and a big "Tanganyika jack" to lift Mzee if necessary.

When the day arrived, I dropped Kabota at his homestead, made a courtesy call on the District Commissioner (suppressing the impulse to tell him I knew Kabota was his spy) and found Harker at the for-

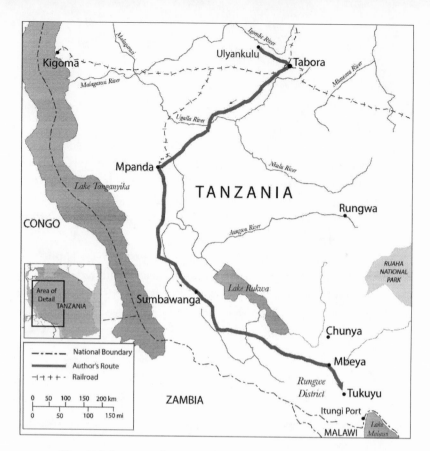

Western Tanzania
Author's route across the Ugalla river to Mpanda and Rungwe District in southwestern Tanzania, 1965. (Map by Ellen Kozak)

estry office. We borrowed a second snakebite kit from the senior forester, and tossed Harker's bedroll into the back of Mzee. The older man was not smiling.

"Come back on schedule, Harker. Plenty of work around here, you know. Remember, the regional report?"

After we had pulled away, Harker turned to me. "You know, Miller, there is a difference between that bloke and me. I'm an Aussie—he's a Limie. I'm a nice guy. He's a buffalo dick…a big pink buffalo dick."

"Forget it," I said. "Forget the buffalo. You are the navigator. Get out your little compass and find the damn Ugalla river—find a place we can cross it."

After Tabora we passed three small villages, but within the hour we were alone on a dirt track, bouncing through mile after mile of desolate bush. Animals often stood transfixed in the track, either because they had not heard Mzee's engine or because they had never seen a vehicle. The first day I counted thirty-four different kinds of birds, dozens

The author's sketch of painted sticks that invoke witchhunt fears and serve as warnings around a honey tree in southwestern Tanzania.

Ugalla track and honey hunter's shelter. (Author's collection)

of impala, four sable antelope, a herd of zebra, dozens of Thomson's gazelle, warthogs, a pack of wild dogs and three small elephants. Several dung beetles rolled their loads across the track, and on three occasions we drove over trains of safari ants. Twice, exhilarated by the wild country, Harker leaned out the window, beat the outside door panel and yelled "Waa-hoooo!" into the wind.

In two long days, on different tracks, the only human we saw was a near-naked honey hunter putting a hive into a tree. He was tall and barefoot, with a G-string around his waist, and when he suddenly saw us, he dropped to the ground and disappeared into the bush. Beyond him was a thatched shelter with other traps, a pan, a ladle and a siphon. Around the honey tree were painted carved sticks.

"I've seen them before," Harker said. "They are warnings called *'fimbos*,' Swahili for stick...protective sticks. The owner draws a circle around the tree, then puts them there to warn others not to steal honey. It's your witchcraft business—'cross this line at great risk.'"

"Just like the lion skulls near Usagari," I said. "Both protective symbols and warnings to potential witches."

Harker had not seen the skulls and didn't want to speculate. "I'm a forester, I do trees," he said. "You, Miller, you do voodoo."

Rebuilding the road with logs on the Ugalla River track. (Author's collection)

On the second day, after getting stuck in deep elephant grass and having to jack the vehicle and rebuild the road with small logs, we reached the banks of the Ugalla. It was a bad moment. Upstream rains had swollen the river, meaning at least a day's wait. There was a small Catholic mission across the water, and after we had opened a tin of meat and ate bread, Harker built a signal fire.

Eventually two figures came to the water's edge. Through the binoculars I could see that both were Europeans, Catholic missionary priests, and one had a rifle slung on his shoulder. They waved and then one pointed to the river and shook his head. The other held his arms up in the air and crossed them.

"They don't want us for tea?" Harker said in a fake British accent. "Oh my, sir, what shall we do?"

In a few minutes they waved again and turned away. Their departure gave me a strange feeling, the sense that I was being abandoned and left alone. I wanted to shout, "Wait, wait. Help us get across," even though crossing was clearly impossible.

Harker didn't seem to care. We moved Mzee to set up a camp on a knoll overlooking the river and he then hiked off to survey trees. I decided to get out a camp chair, watch for new birds and write a few notes. Even on the long drive to the Ugalla river I thought of Mohammadi and her banishment trial. I could still see her face looking back from the bus.

I also realized that Mohammadi's case was like thousands of others across East Africa, a remote incident, unreported and unknown beyond the confines of the village. Her neighbors had taken the law into their own hands and convened an illegal court. The incident happened in the agricultural slack season, between the rains, and after a poor harvest, and I wondered if Mohammadi's trial had had something to do with the season. I knew in some regions the slack season is used to resolve smoldering conflicts.

I also wanted to know more about the way Mohammadi's accusers explained her witchcraft. They relied on old myths, about how animals can be controlled by humans, or about people who can send flies into a child's nose. I wondered if there were a set of standard ideas of a witch, a set of symbols that could be tossed around easily. I vowed to read about religious symbols and see if there were parallels to witchcraft.

In about an hour Harker wandered back into camp, happier and dirtier than when he had left, a scratch from a thorn bush across his cheek. We built a fire, cooked soup, toasted bread, watched the sun set downriver, then flipped a coin to see who got to sleep on the comfortable front seat. Harker lost, called all Yanks "lucky piss-heads" and spread his sleeping bag in the back of the Land Rover. We washed the dishes in the river, then threw a line over a tree branch, hoisted the food high above the ground so as not to attract animals and went to bed. The last thing I heard was Harker muttering "piss-head."

By noon the next day dozens of ripples over small rocks showed the river had fallen. Some parts were shallow enough to cross, but in the middle the stone track disappeared into deeper water. Someone had to check it, and again we flipped a coin to see who would wade across. Harker lost again, and I tied the end of our 50-foot rope around his waist. We both went in until the water was a foot deep, and from there I played him out like a fish.

Harker splashed toward the opposite bank, sank up to his thighs but within forty feet, came up again into shallow water. One of the priests was on the far bank and waved for us to come ahead. We hurried back to the Land Rover, packed the gear and then rigged a rubber hose to keep the exhaust pipe from taking water. As long as we kept traction, we could make it in at least two feet of water.

"Harker is short," I thought to myself. "Hell, his thighs are my knees. No problem. It's shallow enough."

We bumped down the bank, into the water and across little stones. At the deepest point we looked at each other. Mzee was sinking deeper than we had expected and water was coming through the floorboards. The current seemed stronger than when Harker had waded in and the weight of the water was pushing us sideways. When the engine began to sputter Harker leaned out of the window and beat on the door panel with his fist.

"Go, Mzee...you can swim! Go, go! Swim you old bastard!" Mzee must have heard him. It kept chugging, we gained traction, and bumped slowly ahead. There was water around the brake pedal, and the floor under Harker's feet was soaked.

On the bank the priest was clapping and pointing up to the sky as if we had crossed by divine intervention. He turned out to be Father Hugh McFadden from Dublin, about fifty, a slender sun-burned man in bush shorts with a rifle on his shoulder. After we shook hands he invited us to the mission for lunch and a beer. I decided to walk with Father Hugh while Harker drove the dripping Mzee.

"Not wise to wade the river," he said casually in a thick Irish brogue. "Plenty of crocs out there."

"We were only in a few feet of water," I said.

"Oh, a croc can take you in shallow water...even on the bank... that's why the rifle."

We walked a ways in silence. "Let's not tell my friend," I said. "He was out there like bait on a fish line."

Two days later when I dropped Harker at the forestry office in Mpanda town, three African foresters were celebrating the discovery the

"Plenty of crocs out there."

"Miller, you long snout.....
I had a chance to see some woodlands with these blokes and have pushed off for the day. Come see me down under, I'll show you a real croc. Thanks for a good safari, your mate,
—Harker"

Ian Harker
Post 38, Quilipie
Queensland, Australia

day before of a "long snout crocodile" they had captured in the Malagarasi swamp to the north. They claimed it was a species believed extinct. I left Harker in the office to go find fuel, and when I came back there was a note on the door.

It was a sad moment. I wanted to shake hands with Harker, call him a "piss-head," tell him to pat Mzee's fender and say he was sorry for calling the Land Rover a bastard. I wanted to clap him on the back. We had seen a lot together. As I studied the note, something told me our paths would probably not cross again.

I spent five months in Rungwe District and then moved to a coastal village to do research in a fishing culture south of Dar es Salaam. By the time that work ended I had convinced myself it was important to return to western Tanzania to tie up loose ends. The real reason was to find out what had happened to Mohammadi, the banished "witch."

On my way west from Dar es Salaam I stopped at the old railway hotel in Dodoma. This district market town was in the middle of

Gogoland, the area where the British geologist William Hanning had been taken as a witch and speared to death. A friend, Peter Rigby, an anthropologist studying the surrounding Gogo culture, had agreed to meet me at the hotel for a meal. While waiting for Rigby I asked about Hanning, talking first with the bartender, then two waiters and finally the assistant manager. No one remembered him or anything about the case. When Rigby arrived we talked about other things for a while, but over dinner I asked why there was no memory of Hanning. He gave me a quizzical look, then shook his head.

"There is! Of course there is! That was a big event around here, the police were everywhere. William Hanning is just not talked about. A dead witch's name is never mentioned. It would be bad luck to acknowledge him, to remember him, certainly to talk about him."

Rigby lectured me about death beliefs in Gogo culture which he said applied to most Bantu tribal (ethnic) groups. I learned that when good citizens die they are remembered and honored as ancestors. Children memorize their names and deeds, sometimes going back six or eight generations. But, when a witch dies, that person is forgotten and his or her name is erased from the collective memory. It is bad luck to mention the name.

Two days later I parked Mzee under a shade tree in Ibiri, the village to which Mohammadi had been sent. Just as Rigby had foretold, no one acknowledged knowing her until I found an old man named Juma Kabena, a former government messenger who still wore his red fez and a torn khaki shirt. We sat in the village tea shop, and because I had not located Mohammadi, I assumed she had moved away.

"No," Juma said, "She stayed here. The police gave her a hut and a small garden near their post. I knew her. Yes, I knew her, we talked to each other from time to time."

He said she had planted cassava, maize and a few vegetables and kept the four chickens from Usagari. She tried to sell vegetables at the weekly market, but was shunned, by both the market-goers and the other sellers. Elsewhere she was avoided by villagers, particularly women with young children. She rarely spoke to anyone besides Juma.

"Where is she now, where did she go?" I asked.

He gave me a blank look, then shook his head.

"*Pole, bwana* (sorry sir), *pole, pole,*" he repeated.

During the long rains Mohammadi had become ill. The village medic gave her tablets, but told Juma that she had a *shauri za kichwa* (a problem of the head). Juma said she died alone, sitting on the floor of her hut, her arms across her bed. He had helped carry her on the medic's stretcher to the police post. He said her hair was very carefully braided and was very pretty.

"*Kwisha kufa* (she has finished dying). *Kwisha kufa,*" he said.

While we sipped tea, I sketched in my notebook, then pushed it across to Juma.

"Yes, that was how she was," he said.

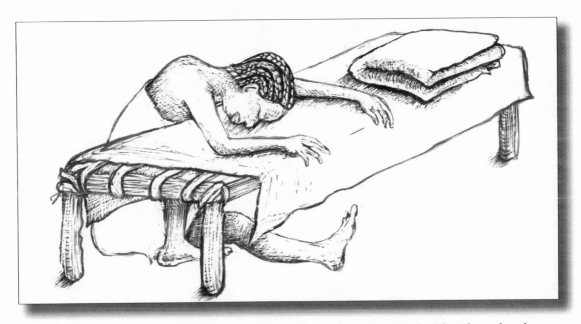

Mohammadi Lupanda's last moments. (Drawing by Eden Abram, based on author's sketch.)

"Was she known by everyone as a witch," I asked.

He didn't asknwer for several moments.

"Yes, all knew, but if she had lived, she would have been accepted…slowly."

"Where is she buried?" I asked. "Is there a marker?"

No, Juma reported, the police buried her behind the supply shed. There was no stone. Her belongings and the four chickens were sent to her brother by bus. As I stood to go, he shook his head again. Two of the chickens, one orange, one black, had been stolen along the way.

A few days later, as I drove back to the coast, I realized that several things still troubled me about the Usagari cases. I did not understand why Mohammadi, apparently so quiet and docile, had been banished as a witch. What else did her neighbors know that had not been revealed at the trial? There had to be some concrete explanation for her plight. There was also a mystery in the chief's poisoning case. If the poison was harmless, as the government lab had indicated, what killed the chief? Nor did I fathom how witchcraft was woven into this culture or how Africans *see* witchcraft—particularly what the images about the beliefs really were.

3

Through African Eyes: The Arts

1966-1967

Chief John Mdeka, Usagari village, Tanzania
Chief Gordon Mwansasu, Magistrate, Rungwe, Tanzania
Barrie Reynolds, Curator, Rhodes-Livingston Museum, Zambia

Earlier in 1966, just before I left Usagari village and before Ian Harker and I splashed across the Ugalla river, Chief John Mdeka came by the compound where I lived. I had invited him to see a copy of an old book by a German missionary priest, Father Boesch, which had drawings of traditional Nyamwezi tools and artifacts. He sat in my canvas chair turning the pages and murmuring "Yes, yes," as he saw things he remembered as a child. The next day he came back, this time with an object wrapped in an oil-stained cloth. He laid it on the table, pushed it towards me and took the cloth away. It was an old Nyamwezi mask. Mdeka slowly pulled two beaded objects from his pockets, put them next to the mask, and looked up. He was not smiling.

Nyamwezi wooden mask, (kifuniko, carved circa 1925), given to the author in Usagari village, Tabora District, Tanzania in 1964. Separate objects made from glass beads, leather straps and cow hair which allowed different configurations on the mask for ritual purposes. (Author's collection)

"These are for you. Take them, Meela (Miller)," he said. "Guard them for us. Nobody here wants them. People no longer believe in the power of masks."

With his elbows on the table, the Chief draped one of the beaded objects over the mask. I sensed he might be worried about giving the things away, perhaps of betraying the ancestors.

"What about one of the museums—the one in Dar is...."

He shook his head. "I know about them. They are corrupt. They will sell it to *wazungu* (Europeans). They won't keep it. You have it, Milla. You keep it."

Chief John said my gift was an execution mask, worn to hide the identity of the person who sentenced someone to die. He reported people were mainly executed for adultery with a chief's wife, and that the condemned were carried to a large outcrop of rocks near Unga hill. There, the tendons in their ankles and legs were slashed with a machete and they were left to the hyenas. It happened at sunset. Usually only a few bones were found the next day.

The beaded objects were called "*kishingo*," and were put on the mask to pronounce sentences for different crimes.

"Why else were people executed?" I asked.

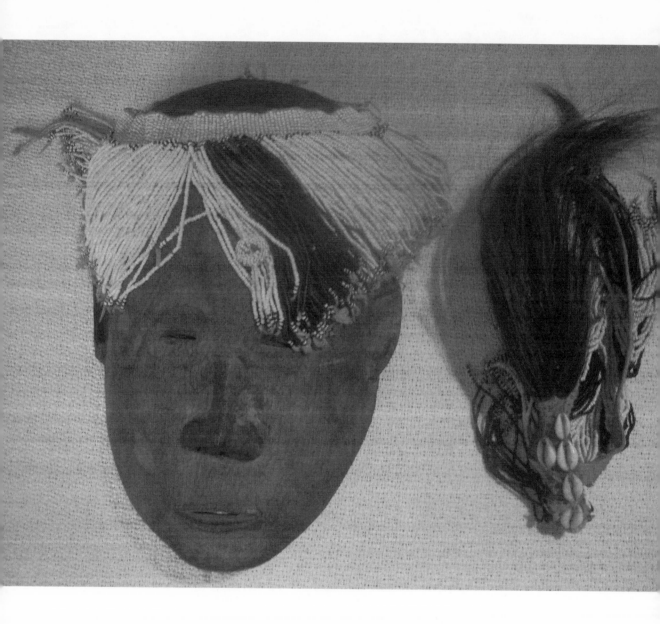

For the first time that afternoon, the chief smiled. "Your subject, Meela. For giving the death sentence to people who practiced witchcraft."

Chief Mdeka remembered how other Nyamwezi masks were used to depict stories, particularly for teaching children or for initiation into secret societies. He said they were meant to shock, to suggest protection against witches whom he described as "people who poison others, do bad things, and can be hired." The chief said his most frightening childhood memories were of witchcraft stories being enacted at night, with drumming and dancing near a big fire, the children made to sit together and keep their heads low to the ground.

"Why low to the ground?" I asked.

"I think to make those who played witches look bigger," he said.

When Mdeka got up to leave he patted the old mask on its nose, then looked at me and took my hand in both of his. "Return here when you can, Meela. Tell us how our mask likes living in your country."

My new mask, plus the lion skulls near Usagari, and the three painted *fimbo* sticks that I had seen on the trip with Ian Harker made me wonder about other items used by alleged witches—the poison containers, carved items, lion claws, and tiny ceremonial spears. I was curious about how Africans see witchcraft and started drawing or photographing anything I ran across.

My new research site in southern Tanzania was in a beautiful, tea- and coffee-growing area just north of Lake Malawi called Rungwe District. Here again the African District Commissioner welcomed me, approved my fieldwork and gave me a stack of papers to read on Rungwe agriculture. I found a village called Sesso, rented a tiny workers' house on the tea estate next to the village and settled down to my research.

The second person I met in Sesso village was another former chief named Gordon Mwansasu. He was the counterpart to ex-Chief John Mdeka in Usagari, but there the similarity ended. Chief Mwansasu had been educated in one of Tanzania's elite secondary schools, sent for administrative training and later, as a young chief, taken to London with a dozen chiefs for Queen Elizabeth's coronation.

He was a thin, bouncy and balding man, forever shaking hands with everyone he met, including children. He had retired two years before as a local court magistrate and, with his wife, now ran a coffee farm and banana grove near my village. He drove a small brown pickup truck, and when walking, carried a tattered briefcase which he claimed had been given to him by the Queen. One afternoon I saw him in Tukuyu town buying supplies and invited him to stop by Sesso village. He came the next afternoon.

"So you want to show me African art?" he said as he climbed out of his pick-up truck. "This will cost you tea and two spoons of sugar." He was smiling, but leaned against the truck until I brought out two canvas chairs, a little camp table and the file of photos.

Rungwe District, Mbeya Region, Tanzania, 1966. (Map by Ellen Kozak)

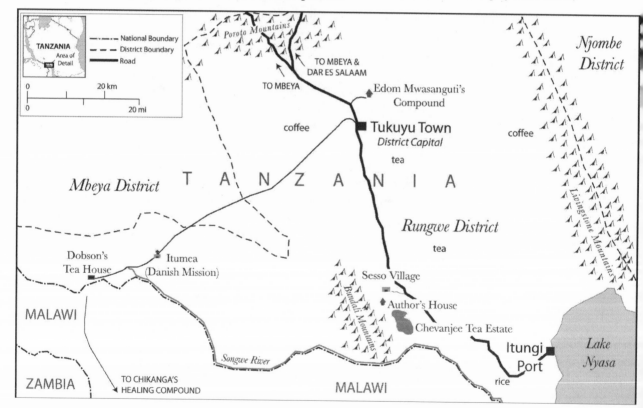

"What am I looking for?" he said, without much interest.

"I'm trying to understand witchcraft." I said. "I want to see witchcraft as Africans do who have grown up with it—through African eyes. This is my own collection of photos and my own sketches about witchcraft. I wonder if you would...."

"I don't believe in witchcraft…" he said with conviction. "It's rubbish, it's destructive and dangerous to old people. We have laws against it." He seemed annoyed, and I struggled to get the conversation back on track. "Chief Gordon, I understand," I said, pouring his tea and pushing the sugar bowl to him. "It is important because so many people get hurt in these witch-hunts. There is a lot of violence in western Tanzania, even on the coast. All over. Even Kenya, even Uganda."

"I want you to know I am *not* a believer," he said. "I'm Christian… more or less."

"I don't believe in witchcraft…"

"Chief, you are my teacher," I said quietly. "I'm trying to understand what Africans believe about witchcraft. It is very confusing because there are so many reports. Can I read you a summary?"

"OK...sure," he said, gesturing for more tea, and now apparently relieved I understood he did not believe in witchcraft.

I hurried inside to get the file, growing uneasy that I was about to tell an African what non-Africans write about a sensitive subject.

"OK," I said. "First, witches are thought to be living people, humans with mysterious powers and bad characters. These "witches" are seen as solitary, selfish, envious, brooding, bad-tempered, cunning and deceitful. They are believed to often roam at night, be able to travel at great speeds, fly or ride on hyenas and be in the neighborhood if someone sees fast-moving lights or distant fires. They rob graves, use human body parts to make medicines, and eat rotten animal flesh, particularly frogs and snakes. They are cannibals."

I paused, took a sip of tea. The chief was watching me intently.

"Witches can make you sick," I continued, "send illness via insects, and injure people without being seen. Witches often have physical defects and disabilities, ugliness, deformity, red or misaligned eyes. They may smell bad. They may have odd manners, odd speech, peculiar behavior and wear outlandish dress.

"In some ethnic groups, witches are thought to be sexual perverts. They may engage in incest, bestiality, sodomy, adultery and homosexuality. They are outsiders—unsociable and devious, the opposite of the ordinary, which may be indicated by images of creatures that are upside down or inside out. They can be traitors, enemies of the people, or political extremists. Ordinary people are expected to be friendly, frugal, and sharing. Witches are the opposite, prone to excess and repugnant behavior."

Chief Gordon sat there, now staring at his teacup. He didn't say anything, but again began to flip through my folder of sketches and photos.

"All right," he finally said. "A lot of those ideas about witches are still around. Some have been dropped, and some are only talked about by elders, and no one group of people believes all that. I think that is a list of traits across East Africa...of the Bantu people, the farmers, not the pastoralists."

I wanted him to say more but at that point he pulled out three photos from my file and laid them on the table. They were the images I had found a year earlier in the gloomy basement of the British Museum, images of witches painted on the walls of a chief's house that were photographed by a colonial officer in 1932. They were taken in a village in the Usambara mountains of northeastern Tanzania. Two of the photos were of witches riding on hyenas wrapped in light bulbs. A third was of a witch standing with birds on her shoulders and a firepot on her head.

"What do you see?" I asked, as he studied the images. "Can you explain what is happening?"

"Yes, I think so," he replied in a hushed voice as if the photos had some power. "These are pictures of witches, as Africans saw them, but they are also warnings to witches to stay away from the chief and his village. They suggest witches can transform themselves into animals, ride on hyenas, and use animals for their work. They show that witches can be upside down—that is, be very abnormal—do the opposite of what is sociable, do evil things. Look at their outlandish clothing, that's proof they are not like others. Sure, a lot of the ideas you just read are here.

"This one," he continued. "This one is proof that witches are cannibals. They have made the hyena get them a human leg. See the leg in its mouth?"

"A lot of those ideas about witches are still around.

Wall paintings from the house of a chief, possibly chief Kujaga of the Shambala culture at Nyantakara location, Pare District, Tanzania, 1932. The fresco-style images are estimated at approximately four feet in height. (courtesy the British Museum, AF/A44/137-139)

"The light bulbs?" I asked.

"Sure...they mean that witches can do mysterious things, like lighting up a string of light bulbs. He kept studying the photos and then continued.

"You say these were taken in 1932? OK, sure, about that time electric generators were being introduced to the rural areas. The Europeans working in the DC's office would have had electric lights. People were

A spirit in human guise named Unonyere.

"Yeah, these are witches, these are the way witches look to Africans."

amazed at the new lights. The person who painted these pictures gave the witches the light bulbs to show their powers."

The chief got up to leave, but then sat down again and began pulling other photos from the file. "You wanted to know what Africans really think witches look like, right? These are good, these are African ideas. These are not a *mzungo's* (European's) idea."

He continued to rummage in the files and then pulled out a half dozen photos. "Yeah, these are witches, these are the way witches look to Africans."

A few minutes later he seemed to get tired of the whole business and picked up some of my own sketches and drawings. A grin crossed his face.

"Who drew these pictures?" he asked.

"I did," I said, not knowing what else to say.

"When you were a little boy?" he asked. "When you were about nine?"

Later during my fieldwork, I learned that many agriculturalists, including farm children, believe witchcraft is proven by odd things in nature. My list included thunder, lightning, prowling animals, weird bird activity and anything abnormal in the behavior of domestic animals. Other evidence of witchcraft was unexpected wind, sudden hailstorms, oddly formed tufts of grass or sticks lying in strange ways on the ground. The sighting of certain wild animals was believed to indicate witchcraft was being practiced nearby—the python among the Nyakyusa people where I was living, the owl in Baganda, the hyena among the Nyamwezi and Sukuma. In spite of Chief Gordon's comments, I continued to make sketches.

During a research trip I made to Zambia, the curator of the Rhodes-Livingston Museum, Barrie Reynolds, suggested that for eastern and central Africa, some artifacts related to witchcraft might be called a "witch's toolkit." These were items used by people who *claimed* to be witches or who used certain items commonly believed to have witchcraft powers. Grave robbing implements, certain botanical plants,

Through African Eyes—What Witches Look Like

Seven images that exemplified an African chief's view of what witches look like (Chief Gordon Mwansasu, Rungwe District, Tanzania, 1967). Several of the illustrations were created by unknown African informants for the government sociologist Hans Cory in the 1930s and related to mythical figures of terror in snake charming groups of the Sukuma-Nyamwezi people. They include:

(A) Spirit image with snake.
(B) A twin-headed giant named Simungala.
(C) A figure of a woman who sat on arrows.
(D) A human-bird figure, Niangalima.
(E) A woman who saw fire emanating from the anus of her sister.
(F) A Makonde spirit carving.
(G) A shetani spirit carving typical of Makonde art form.

(Photo opposite page and (A) to (E) above, Hans Cory Collection, University of Dar es Salaam. Photo (F)author's collection.) Photo (G) Jesper Kirknaes collection.

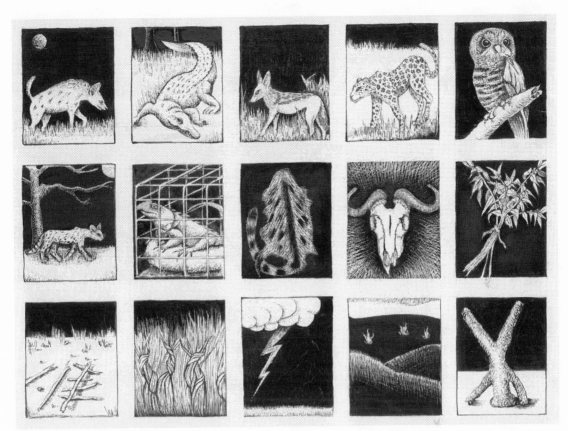

Natural Symbols That Represent Witchcraft   *Paraphernalia to promote beliefs in witchcraft : Upper left to right: hyena, crocodile, jackal, leopard, owl. Second row: civet cat, caged reptile, animal skin, animal skull, certain botanical plants. Third row: randomly scattered sticks, tied tufts of grass, distant lightning, distant fires, inverted clay or wood figures. (Drawings after author's sketches by Eden Abram)*

animal skins, fetishes, flywhisks, lion claws, even a tiny plastic skull and toy rubber crocodile were some of the items. Other "tools" included human hair, fingernail clippings, unidentified bones and ashes from someone's fire—all things thought to have power to bewitch.

As I had learned from the crocodile hunter, Eric van der Whipple, even items that only suggested witchcraft was being done nearby could be used for intimidation—a kind of "power of suggestion"

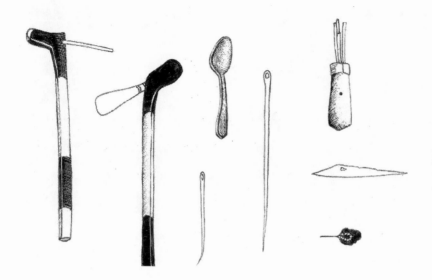

Grave-Robbing Tools
From left, digging hoe, axe, spoon, small probing needle, large needle, needles in sheath, knife blade, sewing needle set in beeswax. Tools may also be used in secret ceremonies and ritual feasts and as symbolic displays. (Drawing by Eden Abram)

or placebo effect. Red powders delivered in an envelope, discolored needles apparently dipped in poison and put in someone's pathway, thorns that could be covered in poison found near where one urinates, are examples. Other threatening items include blood of a cobra smeared on a piece of wood left on a bed, animal excrement on a leaf found just inside a house, or a tiny carved figure half-buried near a doorway. Many items, like skulls or ritual knives were kept secret and only displayed as a show of power or when demanding a price to intimidate someone's enemy. I made sketches or took photos of some of these items whenever they turned up in my fieldwork, and labeled them the "witch's toolkit."

Both the natural items that symbolized witchcraft and some of the items in the witch's toolkit reminded me of the trial of Mohammadi in Usagari village. She supposedly sent insects to harm the baby who died, brought hyenas to the village and wore red cloth. Chief Mwansasu made me realize that these things were symbols that led people to believe that witchcraft was around. I puzzled for a long time over how this process works and finally decided the symbols such as

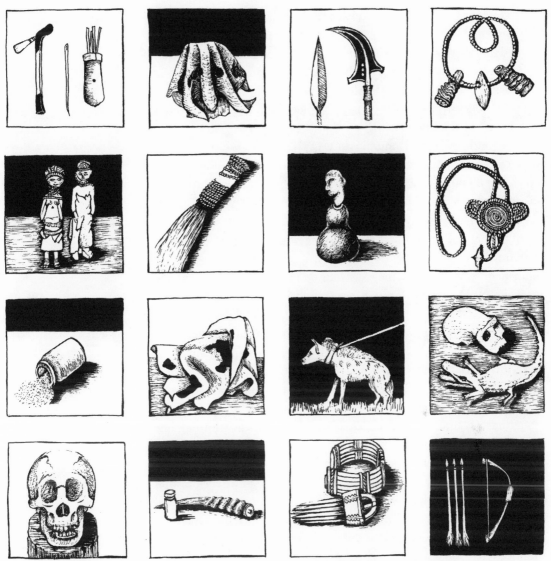

Items in a Witch's Toolkit   *Paraphernalia, from upper left: grave digging tools, red cloth, ceremonial throwing knives or spear, wrist amulets. Second row: small carved figures, arm band, carved medicine container, beaded ornament. Third row: medicine in a container, oiled rag, leashed animal, rubber or plastic small figures. Fourth row: human skull, "magical" medicines, strange bracelet or emblem, tiny bow and arrow. (Drawing by Eden Abram)*

a red cloth or a wild animal, were "code" items. When seen or verbally hinted at, they served as a shorthand way to call up old myths. I decided that there were at least four basic myths underlying witchcraft.

One was a *transformation* myth—the suggestion that humans can transform themselves into animals. This was part of the "shape-shifting" idea, known in mythology since ancient times. The "lion-men" murder cases I ran into on my first trip were examples.

A second key myth I pinpointed was *predation*—the belief that a witch can control things that prey upon you: wild beasts, huge snakes, things that eat humans, a key nightmare throughout the world. My third was the *inversion* myth found in many cultures. Here the idea is that witchcraft is evidenced by things upside-down or inside-out. The opposite of the natural, the normal, the expected. Finally, I decided that *pollution* myths were important—that witches cause filth, dirt, grotesque abnormalities, for example the ideas found in some Makonde carvings.

There were obviously other ways symbols were used to suggest witchcraft ideas and I decided to lay out my four symbolic categories to Chief Gordon. He was used to thinking about the law in abstract terms but here he shook his head. "Careful with this symbolism business," he said. "It is a swamp, Miller, if you go very far you may never return."

Chief Gordon liked the "witch's toolkit" idea but made a further distinction. He said most villagers see witchcraft as both offensive, that is things that can attack them, and defensive, things that can protect them. He gently suggested I should have figured this out for myself.

"It is an important distinction. Remember, I was a magistrate fourth class," he said, tapping his briefcase. "Those things—powders, poisons, bones rags, diviners kits—were all brought to my court to try to prove violation of the witchcraft ordinance. We had to sort out what was intended to hurt someone—that is your "offensive" things—and what was meant to protect—the "defensive" healer's things. I see these things as either offensive or defensive."

We were at my little house on the tea estate and Chief Gordon asked for the file of photos and sketches he had seen before.

"Sure, defensive things are important," he repeated. "They can be good-luck charms, wooden carvings, clay figures, these beads, even some of the stone carvings. They are defensive, for good luck. They are found at all levels in African society."

"Levels?" I asked.

"Of course. Take the amulets...they can be for a baby's protection or an individual's good luck—things carried in the pocket. These carved figures can be for a family shrine, for protection. Your mask, the wall paintings, the lion skulls, a chief's ritual hut are for village protection. A healer's collection of decorated gourds for medicine is very defensive, very symbolic. And there is even a higher level. Some African nations put pictures, masks or images on their money or stamps, which suggests the state has occult power. For some people this means the state can protect people against witchcraft–that it has special power. Find some of the money from West Africa or the Congo, you will see."

Defensive Objects Against Witchcraft
Examples of defensive objects against witchcraft for a family or a community include, top row from left, a carved Chief's stool with protective motifs, (Nyamwezi), wall hangings and special bead work. From lower left, a boar's tooth and monkey paws worn by a baby for protection, a wooden carved figure for a house or chief's compound, and an ornate carved and beaded medicine stick with carved stopper. (Drawings after author's sketches by Eden Abram)

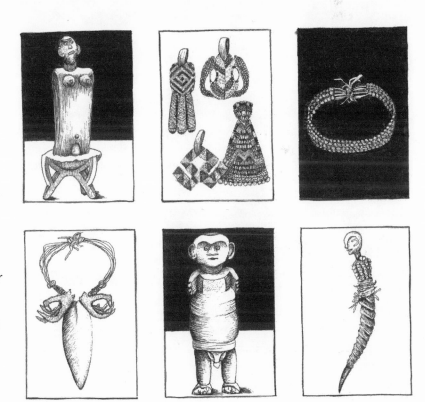

Decorative gourds for medicine in a healer's clinic serve as defensive or protective symbols. They allow storage of leaves, bark, stems as well as prepared compounds. (British Museum. AF/B19/35)

While in Zambia I had made sketches of another kind of defensive witchcraft weapon that I thought would not be known to anyone in southern Tanzania. These were home-made guns and again I misjudged Chief Mwansasu. As I showed him my sketches he nodded.

"Of course," he said. "There are defensive things, rare around here, but they are *kilogozi* guns from Zambia, maybe some in Malawi. They are the biggest protective weapons a village can use against a suspected witch."

Traditional Kiligozi guns from Zambia were made from pipe or human bone, lashed to wooden stocks and sealed with beeswax. They shot tiny hard peas, stones or pieces of metal with explosions of gunpowder set off with a match. Their main function is to instill terror and thus deter suspected witches from practicing. (Drawing by Eden Abram after original sketches from Barrie Reynolds, Rhodes-Livingston Museum, Zambia.)

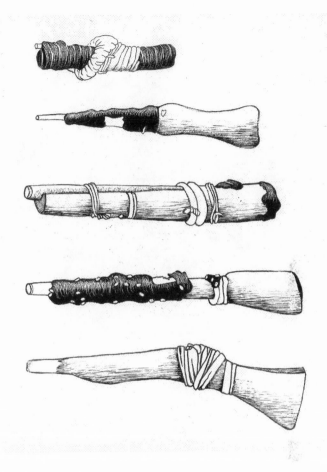

Chief Gordon suggested two other kinds of witchcraft material that I should look for: "teaching devices" and "power symbols." He suggested I first find items like clay dolls used to teach children about witchcraft and carvings or clay figures a grandfather might use to teach a folktale about witches.

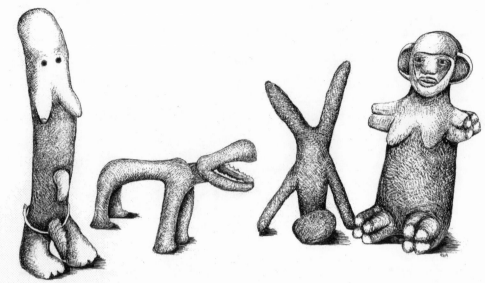

Clay figures were used in several East African ethnic groups for teaching about witchcraft. (Drawing by Eden Abram)

The things Chief Gordon called "power symbols" were objects used to create awe and respect. Some served multiple roles: they were power symbols and protective symbols at the same time. Examples included the 1932 chief's wall frescos from the Usambara mountains. Others were "power items" like throwing knives found in northern Uganda and the Sudan, used by healers to show status and power, and the protective Nyamwezi chief's throne with carvings to ward off witchcraft and bad fortune or the ritual hut near where I slept in Usagari village. I knew that West Africa and the Congo region historically produced elaborate power symbols for lodges and secret societies and I showed the chief one image I had found earlier. He studied it at length.

"This is real power," he said. "We don't have these around here, but look at the attention to details, bones, animal skulls, carved pieces. This thing establishes the group's authority, demands attention, commands obedience. And of course it plays on all the supernatural fears you talk about. There would be dozens of stories tied to it, I'm sure, like the Christian carvings in the great cathedrals. This thing is a real African power figure, just not out of our corner of Africa."

Other power items common to East Africa included an array of objects and could be unique to a very specific region. Throwing knives, for example, once used in combat in the Sudan, the northeastern Congo and northern Uganda to bring down horses have been used by contemporary healers and diviners in northern Uganda to show status and power. Wrist and finger knives have the same role.

Elsewhere in the region walking sticks, funeral sticks, flywhisks, and a wide array of carved masks carried meaning, established authority, demanded attention and stood as proof of individual status. Outside wall art was a power symbol in several regions.

Throwing knives.
(Drawing by Eden Abram)

A late 19th century power emblem from the Ekpe society, Banyang peoples in the Cameroon/Nigeria border areas. Made of raffia, animal skulls and wood, (height 120. cm, width 102.2 cm). (Used by the permission of the owner.)

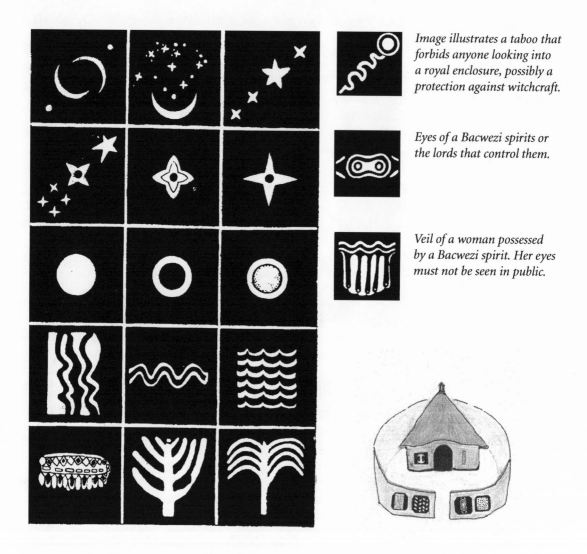

Image illustrates a taboo that forbids anyone looking into a royal enclosure, possibly a protection against witchcraft.

Eyes of a Bacwezi spirits or the lords that control them.

Veil of a woman possessed by a Bacwezi spirit. Her eyes must not be seen in public.

The Hima people in southwestern Uganda, cousins of the Ankole, traditionally used wall paintings on their houses and exterior walls as decorative art forms and in some cases as symbols of power. Images from the 1930s and 1940s depicted in an article by C.M. Sekintu and K.P. Wachsmann, "Wall Patterns in Hima Huts." (Kampala: The Uganda Museum Paper No. 1, 1956). Also see Fountain Publishers publications on Hima art, 1966, 2012. The Hima wall paintings were used like Egyptian hieroglyphics to convey ideas, and were not part and parcel of witchcraft beliefs. They may also be seen as power symbols like the other items portrayed. A few Hima paintings referred to spirits and spirit possession. They all may be compared to the wall paintings for specific witchcraft protection, as seen on page 84-85. Hut sketch by Ben Kozak.

On a bright sunny day in the Tukuyu town tea house, Chief Gordon shattered all the neat categories I had used to organize my witchcraft sketches. We were talking about dividing witchcraft objects into offensive vs. defensive items.

"Of course most of these things are interchangeable," he said with the look of someone who knew everything. "Those ideas that the offensive 'witches' toolkit' is the opposite of the 'protective or defensive toolkit' is wrong—the items can be the same things. They can be interchangeable. Those artifacts and fetishes—almost everything—can be *anything* the owner says they are. It is the healers or the avowed witch who give them power."

"Help!" I said. "I don't understand. *You* set up this offensive versus defensive business because of your courtroom—you told me...."

He paid no attention. "The practitioners—good or bad—give the items their power," he said. "Like one of these local church people waving a cross and shouting 'God is here.' The cross has symbolic power. But it is the people's beliefs...that's where the power comes from."

"They are mostly symbols?" I asked.

"Of course they are symbols. Only the poisons and the weapons— they are not symbols. They can hurt people. The rest of the things are symbols, they are part of the language of witchcraft. When you understand how that works, you'll understand a lot more about Africans."

"The language of witchcraft?" I said. "I think that's what I'm trying to understand."

Chief Gordon didn't hear me. He had turned around and was shaking hands with people at the next table.

Later that year, in New York, on the way home from this research trip, my interest in African art led me to a pretty girl from Oklahoma named Judith von Daler. She worked at the Museum of Modern Art and on the side ran a small private gallery of Zimbabwe stone sculptures. Even when she told me my idea that the stone carvers used witchcraft ideas to create their art was vague and a bit silly, something told me the search for the perfect woman had come to an end.

4

Witch-Hunters and Witch-Cleansers

1969

Edom Mwasanguti, witch-hunter, witch-cleanser, Tanzania
Eugen Schneider, Swiss tea estate manager, Tanzania
Birgit Nielson, Danish missionary, Rungwe District, Tanzania
Dobson Mwaipopo, hotel keeper, Malawi border
Leighton Chunda, "Chikanga," healer, Rumpi, Malawai
Kabwere Wangi, witch-cleanser, Kenya coast
Tsuma Washe, "Kajiwe," witch-hunter, Kenya coast

Witch-hunting in sub-Saharan Africa is a big business. I had vaguely known this, but it was my friend Chief Gordon Mwansasu in Rungwe District who began my education on this topic. He gave me a handwritten note to Edom Mwasanguti, a witch-hunter. "He is famous in this region... very powerful," the chief said. "He is fearless against people who could hurt him or poison him...and he is very controversial."

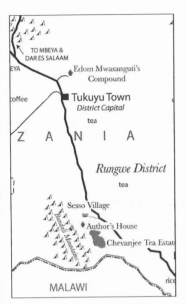

Location of compound of Edom Mwasanguti, Rungwe District

"Controversial?" I asked.

"You'll learn. Go meet him. He's north of Tukuyu town, four or five miles on the Itagata road...anyone up there can direct you."

The next day, when I found Edom Mwasanguti, he was reclining in an old wooden chair, watching his three grandchildren play with a baby chicken. He stood to welcome me, a tall man with piercing eyes, dressed in a khaki shirt and shorts.

"I heard the vehicle," he said after he read Chief Gordon's note. "I'm glad you're not that Moravian missionary trying to convert me—again."

Yes, we could talk, but first he asked if he could have a ride to town when we finished. He then sent one of his grandchildren to get a folder and carefully filed my note.

Edom Mwasanguti was born near Tukuyu town. He told me he had been educated for nine years in a nearby mission school, and then worked there as a carpenter. He began selling herbs and then witch-hunting in his mid-forties, and he boasted that now he would challenge anyone to overpower him with witchcraft. He added that a year ago he had gone to Dar es Salaam to offer his witch-hunting services to the Tanzanian government.

"Even Kasambala, my MP from here, helped me," he continued. "And we went to see the Vice President, Rashidi Kawawa. I told him I wanted to hunt witches for Tanzania, to help the country."

"What happened?" I asked, thinking I would hear a success story.

"Nothing!" Edom exclaimed, obviously annoyed. "The VP turned us down. He even wrote a circular against me!" He rummaged in the same file brought by his grandson. "Maybe you can help me get this reversed," he said, as he handed me a government circular.

> VP directs that the Regional Commissioners should be reminded that all belief in witchcraft, all practice, whether white or black, is a criminal offense under the witchcraft ordinance. It would be highly embarrassing to Government if we on the one hand prosecute witches and on the other used witchcraft.
>
> Permanent Secretary
> Vice President's Office, Dar es Salaam

"Maybe you can get this reversed," he repeated.

"Let's talk about it next time," I said. "Let's talk again."

Over the next few months I visited Edom's compound several times to watch and photograph public "witch-cleansing." Our agreement was that I would give him photos in exchange for explanations of his techniques.

Over those weeks I learned that Edom was not like the religious prophets who witch-hunted for a sect or church. He claimed no particular religious calling or medical expertise. He was secular, a traditional practitioner who saw witches as malicious social deviants, not sinners against a religious creed. Normally he would be called to a distant village and offered a fee to reveal who was responsible for a tragedy and was thus a witch. First he would set up a camp and a cooking fire near the village and then recruit several teenage boys. He provided food, *pombe* (beer) and sometimes *bhang* to smoke. Late night discussions with the boys revealed who the villagers already suspected.

In the first witch-cleansing ceremony I watched, Edom was dressed like a British colonial officer in knee socks, safari shorts and a field hat, a uniform he said that gave him status because he looked like an official. That day he spoke to the crowd about the importance of peace and village unity. I noticed he had adopted many of the ideas of "keeping a peaceful compound" from the nearby Safwa people, ideas that resonated with the local Nyakyusa. He then spoke directly to the "witches" present, daring them to hurt him and demanding their confessions.

"I know you are there! I know who you are! You cannot hide!" he shouted in a stentorian voice. "Now, now...try to hurt me...try your magic on me now!" he shouted, his voice rising as he unbuttoned his shirt and stuck out his chest. "I know who you are!"

The boys who had revealed the names of suspected witches were sent running through the village to look for "witchcraft medicines." Because most people kept unmarked medicine containers—little cans, gourds or bottles—in the roof thatch of their huts, such things were easy to find. None were labeled, and only the owners knew their contents. Identification of the ingredients in the containers was impossible without a lab test.

"Now, now...
try to hurt me...
try your magic
on me now!"

The objects were laid before Mwasanguti who identified them as "witchcraft substances." The owners of the containers were then summoned and accused of practising witchcraft. They were the exact people that the boys had told Edom about earlier.

"How did you know which medicines belonged to the suspects?" I asked when we discussed a ceremony. Edom answered with remarkable candor.

"I pay the boys. When they lay the medicine of their suspect before me, they tap it three times with their finger. They had given me the name earlier. Each boy had only one suspect. I smell the medicine and identify it as bad,...then accuse the owner as a 'witch'."

"What happens then ?" I asked.

"I call out all their names again...out loud. I call them witches. I invite them to try to hurt me. I lecture them. I say that I know they may *not* be aware of their witchcraft, but that it was they who had caused the village problems—maybe unconsciously."

Although it did not happen in the ceremony I watched, Edom told me that he usually closed his part of the public meeting by offering to cleanse anyone who cared to confess in a ceremony—at his compound. Before leaving, he would praise the village elders for their courage and, because he had secretly been paid earlier, he could leave with fanfare.

Edom admitted that some of these meetings led to violence, especially after he had left the village and names of the accused circulated throughout the village. Most of the time, however, the suspects confessed on the spot and asked to come to his compound for a cleansing ceremony. After this ceremony the cleansed person would be accepted back into the community. He also offered ceremonies for people who needed protection or feared they had witchcraft within them. The cost to the individuals could be paid in shillings, farm produce such as eggs or coffee beans, or by indenturing a daughter to work in Mwasanguti's banana plots.

"Come next week, Thursday at 4:00," he said when we parted. "Bring Chief Gordon. You can see another ceremony. Yes...bring Chief Gordon."

> *"I call them witches. I invite them to try to hurt me."*

The opening ceremony of a witch-cleansing ritual with Edom Mwasanguti (back to camera) and an assistant. Both men are dressed in colonial officer attire with bush jackets, knee socks, safari hats and walking sticks. (Author's collection)

Edom taps the chest of a possessed woman.

Woman ostensibly possessed by spirits.

Edom with his exhibit of "witchcraft medicines" found in the homes of alleged practitioners.

Detail of exhibit containers: gourds with stoppers, goat horns with plugs, 35-mm film cans, glass bottles, oil cans, fetishes containing medicines made with cow's tails.

Closing ceremony with singing led by Edom with young women presenting ceremonial gifts (eggs) to those who confessed.

When I passed on Edom's invitation to Chief Gordon, he was definitely not interested. "The man is dangerous," Gordon said. "The new Area Commissioner is worried about him. He has caused people to get hurt. There was real violence in Upuge last year—mob violence against those he accused as witches. He also may be abusing the young girls, the daughters sent to him to pay debts."

"He wants me to write a letter to the government to support his witch-finding—to allow him to keep the peace," I said, watching the chief carefully.

"Don't do it. You could get into trouble and lose your research clearance. There are a lot of these people in Tanzania. Most are exploiters." It was one of the few times I saw Chief Gordon angry.

"Look at Mwasanguti!" he said. "He goes to a village, names witches, then gets them to come to his compound for cleansing *and* to pay him for his services."

"Big business," I said.

"Big racket," Gordon replied shaking his bald head.*

Chief Gordon also taught me the distinction between witch-

* Edom Mwasanguti used the same system the diviner Hamisi Ali and his assistant Jamal used in Usagari during the trial of Mohammadi. They confirmed what everybody already thought and made a profit in the process.

hunting and witch-cleansing. Witch-hunters "name" witches. Cleans-ers simply "purify" those who are accused or who believe themselves bewitched. Some, like Edom, do both. The chief told me that the best known public cleansings in the region were in the shaving salons near Iringa, Tanzania. Among the Hehe people busloads of individuals went to have their heads shaved in a peaceful ritual. If their problem was based on a conflict between neighbors or within a family, often both parties went for shaving at the same time. Chief Gordon held the Hehe up as a model because of this peaceful conflict resolution.

Through the chief I also learned how a witch-cleanser can use his powers to extort money.

"Sure," Chief Gordon said as we bounced along in his little brown truck. "There is a lot of extortion when people believe someone has witch-cleansing powers."

"Extortion by a witch-cleanser? How does that work?"

"Extortion by a witch-cleanser?" I said. "How does that work?"

The chief was still thinking about my question when we came around a curve in the road. He stepped on the brake and pulled over to a man cutting grass near a tethered cow.

"Famous cow," Gordon said. "Let's see how it feels."

I thought he had forgotten my question. Gordon got out, shook hands with the herdsman, and talked for a few minutes. He patted the cow on its nose, wiped his wet hand on the cow's neck and climbed back in the truck.

"Witchcraft extortion case for you," he said. "Gwasobile here was brought to my court. He claimed a healer from Mpuguso abducted his wife and then threatened to hurt him with witchcraft unless he paid a cow—that cow there. Extortion to get his wife back. That's what Gwa-sobile claimed."

"What happened?" I asked, looking back to see the cow.

"Gwasobile went to the police and they set up a trap. The healer was arrested while taking the cow. He was brought to court. Part of the legal issue was whether the healer used or threatened witchcraft in the attempted extortion."

Gordon looked over to see if I was paying attention. "I threw the case out. We never got to the witchcraft charge. Under examination, Gwasobile's wife admitted she had *not* been abducted at all, but ran away with the healer. He seduced her, or maybe she seduced him. Anyway, I made him post a bond to keep the peace, and lectured her about adultery."

Gordon shifted into low gear and drove around a herd of goats. "Isn't that a case where a witchcraft threat is used for extortion?" he said.

Another famous witch-cleanser in Rungwe was a man called Fyala. He made money helping politicians win office and I learned of him soon after I rented a tea worker's run-down house on the edge of Chevanjee tea plantation. The estate manager was a Swiss national named Eugen Schneider and one evening he drove out through the tea bushes to invite me to a "political rally."

"Come tomorrow. You will see real African politics in action. We will use your voodoo to make it exciting."

"Voodoo? Exciting?" I said.

"Sure. We will have Fyala, the 'witch-doctor,' to convince the workers to vote as we tell them."

The meeting the next day was held 24 hours before the national parliamentary elections, and Schneider was promoting the incumbent, Jeremiah Kasambala. At the time the region was rich in tea and coffee, and many of the big estates were owned by British or Swiss companies. European tea managers saw Kasambala as an ally against stricter labor laws the government planned to impose, and hoped for his re-election. The Chevanjee rally was a mass meeting for some 400 workers, mostly tea pickers.

After two speeches by African politicians and a harangue by Eugen Schneider that supported Kasambala, the tea manager laughingly suggested the "witch-doctor" standing with him would reveal the names of anyone who voted against Kasambala. He joked again that he and other tea managers would "not be happy if you don't support Jeremiah." Nobody laughed. Fyala then told the audience he had the ability to know, even foretell, how a person votes, even in a closed booth.

When the rally was over, the estate trucks were impounded and the gates locked to discourage anyone from going to the police to complain. Workers were encouraged to relax in their quarters and be ready to vote at the Rutanganio school early the next morning. In spite of secret voting booths, the final tally was 395 to 6 in favor of Kasambala. Schneider said he thought he knew the dissenters and planned to "sack the buggers."

The next evening, after a reception for Kasambala and other local officials on his flower-decked veranda overlooking far-distant Lake Malawi, Schneider asked what I thought of his "political work." By then I knew him pretty well.

"You rigged the damn election," I said. "What happened to the secret ballot? What happened to democracy? It flew out the window when you intimidated those people. And, how can you be sure you are sacking the right people?"

Schneider was still smiling, clearly pleased with himself. "Everybody talks and gossips, especially the tea-picking girls I bring to the

Influence-peddling during an open-air election, Rungwe, Tanzania. (Author's collection)

house to screw. They will tell me. I think I know the bastards anyway." He paused and poured himself a tumbler of Beehive brandy. "None of them—no one in Africa—is ready for your kind of democracy anyway. That's for god-damn sure. And I'm not the only tea planter around here who knows that."

A few months later I watched Fyala, the same "witch-doctor" who had been on the tea estate, offer advice at a local council election. At this community level, elections were not secret, but open-air: people simply lined up behind their candidate. When the shifting and shuffling stopped, a local election official counted the votes. In this particular election I watched Fyala move among the crowd suggesting his powers let him know the best candidates. That day two of Fyala's cousins and his uncle were running for the Council. All were elected.

While I was still in Rungwe District, a healer and witch-cleanser in nearby Malawi interested me because his reputation had spread so far into southern Tanzania. He was Leighton Chunda, also known as Chikanga. To learn about him I drove toward the Malawi border in the Ndali area and inquired at Itumea in a clinic run by Danish missionaries.

The older nurse, a large, powerful woman called Lene, knew Chikanga, but said she did not like his exploitation of the sick and dismissed my interest as a bad idea. When she went into the clinic, the younger nurse, Birgit Nelson, lingered on the porch, patting her dog, Igor. She quietly helped me.

"Go to the border crossing," she whispered. "You will find a tea house there. A man named Dobson runs it. He will help if you buy a lot of his cakes."

I was struck by her beauty, and I wanted to ask her why she was stuck way out here in very remote Ndali at the Itumea mission. Before I could say anything the older nurse, Lene, appeared in the clinic door.

"Birgit!" she barked. "There is a patient here."

We shook hands and I told her if she wanted to run away from Lene the lion I would help her. She looked interested and asked me to

Near Itumea mission Bundali Hills, Rungwe District, Tanzania.

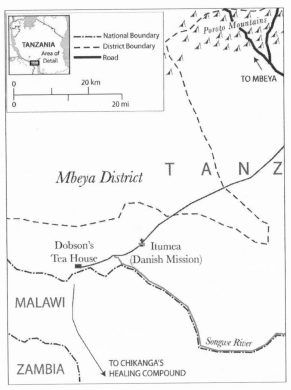

Route to Chicanga's compound Malawi-Tanzania Border area.

write her very soon. The big one was standing in the doorway again as I turned on the engine and waved out the window.

"Mzee is sorry to leave you. He likes it here."

"Who is Mzee?" Birgit said

"The Land Rover. It talks to me."

"Oh my," she said with a Danish lilt and another pretty smile. "How long have you been in the bush? I think you go out in the sun too much!"

Closer to the Malawi border, the dirt track ended and only a narrow path wound into the forest. I parked, asked directions then walked about a mile to a rickety tea house surrounded by grass shelters where travelers en route to Chikanga's compound could sleep and buy food.

Dobson Mwaipopo, the manager, was a convivial middle-aged man. He was Nyakyusa from Tukuyu town, but had a Malawian wife; they lived just across the border where the bus stopped. I watched while he sold tea and cakes, and every now and then filled out a 3-by-5-inch card after talking to customers. He was reluctant to speak at first, but when I bought a bag of cakes, he explained that Chikanga paid him for the cards. Each was a description of an individual en route to see the healer. The cards were sealed in packets of 30 and carried to Chikanga by a teenager on the bus.

Once at Chikanga's compound, a patient was expected to wait a day or two before treatment, stay in the healer's shelters and buy food and medicines. Chikanga's helpers moved among the patients giving advice and collecting further information. Told to remain silent in the healer's presence, the patient would then be shown in to meet a smiling Chikanga dressed in dapper European clothes, reclining on a couch. Chikanga would then tell the patient his own name, his home village, and something about his ailments. The healer often used hands-on healing, gently clutching patients by the neck or holding their hands, sometimes tapping their chest. Appointments lasted about ten minutes and usually ended with confident assurances of a healthy outcome. Many were instructed to return the next day, and most did. Nearby missionaries believed the key to the treatment was the advance information Chikanga had about the person. Most patients believed Chikanga had supernatural healing power—obvious from his knowledge of their personal details.

Dobson said Chikanga did not charge fees, unlike most healers, and very few people connected the food, the medicine and the bus— which Chikanga owned—to him directly. The nearby Christian missionaries, however, did make the connection and, like Lene the lion, had begun to criticize the healer for extortion.

Chikanga's reputation drew thousands of people from Tanzania,

Herbalist Wanjiru (Daily Nation, *Nairobi, Kenya*)

Zambia and Malawi, nearly all swearing by his counsel and medicines. Even when his card scheme became known, his reputation continued to grow. Anthropologist Allison Redmayne, who studied Chikanga, believed his basic secret was to convince patients that he possessed extraordinary spiritual power. It helped that his advice was general enough that anyone could find comfort in what he said.

⸭

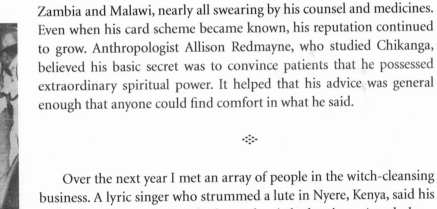

Over the next year I met an array of people in the witch-cleansing business. A lyric singer who strummed a lute in Nyere, Kenya, said his songs offered protection and solace to bewitched patients. A snake handler in a Nairobi hotel lobby said that for a fee the reptile could create a protective, anti-witchcraft aura for me.

A faith healer, Mary Agasta, whose mass healing ceremony I watched in the Kisumu football stadium, used her "powers from god"

Mary Agasta, faith healer (Daily Nation)

Healers who protect against witchcraft: (A) A Kenyan lyric singer; (B) A Nairobi snake handler; (C) John Akunga, Kenyan foreteller brought to the USA by the promoters of the Baltimore Orioles to cast spells on the Boston Red Soxs and predict game scores. (He failed in both assignments.); (D) street healers in Kenya. Photo (A), courtesy of Charles M. Good, Jr. All others, Daily Nation, Nairobi)

to cleanse witchcraft from among hundreds of followers. At one point she was so popular and her followers so boisterous that the government declared her a security risk.

In the back streets of Dar es Salaam, I watched a public *ngoma* (healing ceremony) for a woman whose family and neighbors paid healers to cleanse her of witchcraft. In a Nairobi market I was able to interview a young mother named Wanjiru, who told me she rose before dawn and went to Thika forest to collect herbs that protected people against witchcraft. When I asked her how they worked, she gave me a shy smile. "You must walk in the forest…you must know their power… the herbs have power, you know…you must learn to believe…then you will know."

A few months after meeting Wanjiru I was driving along the Kenya coast near Malindi when I saw a sign that suggested Kabwere Wanje might have something to teach me. He was reluctant at first, but when I brought him a fish from the Malindi wharf he ushered me past rows of herbs and bottles of medicine to the back of the building to talk.

He told me he was a witch-cleanser who used the medicines, often in ceremonies on the beach and often on people who believed they were possessed by *shetani* spirits. Most clients followed a mixture of Islam and traditional Bantu beliefs, but he also treated local African Christians.

"This witchcraft is in all religions," he said. "It cuts like a *panga* (machete) across the villages. I am here, like my father Wanje, to make peace, and to keep *shambas* (households) from fighting. I am not political, like Kajiwe."

Kabwere referred to Tsuma Washe or Kajiwe (Little Stone), who then worked mainly on the Kenya coast. When I found him in his "clinic" near the Mariakani bus stop on the Nairobi-Mombasa road, he had just come from jail. Probably because of this he was willing to talk openly.

"It was very unfair," he said. "I was detained for mixing politics and oathing…for turning my home into an oathing center. None of that is true. I only get people to swear against witches…not against the government."

Kabwere Wanje, near Malindi, Kenya (Author's collection)

He rummaged on his desk for several press clippings. "Look what I do. I find lost children, I give people protection, I solve village problems, I point out the witches, bring peace. And this Moi government—they are like *kukus* (chickens), running everywhere at once, saying anything. Last year they praised me and sent me to Rubai to calm the people. But this year! This year, these *kukus* put me in jail for the same things." He reached for a handkerchief and dramatically blew his nose.*

Later that year, in Kampala, Uganda, my neat distinction between *witch-hunter* and *witch-cleanser* fell apart. At Makerere I was introduced to Charity Masembe, a student who had written a thesis on witchcraft in her home area, near Kabale in southwestern Uganda. We sat on a bench outside the library while Charity politely listened to my theories about witch-hunters and witch-cleansers being quite different.

"Oh, that's *not* how it is in my part of Uganda. It is more complicated," she said, wrinkling her nose and shaking her head. She began to tap lightly on her bound thesis. "In the Bantu vernacular language in my home area there is a word for a special kind of witch, a night dancer who eats human flesh. It's *omusezi*. There is another witch who is a psychological terrorist who prowls at night and makes strange noises, the *omuchraguzi*. Then there is the poisoner—*omurogi*. And others. A lot of others."

"Names for very specific people?" I said. "Those who carry out witchcraft?"

She nodded. "Sure, and on the other side, the good healer with special powers—that's an *omufumu*. There is a touch doctor, the *omumungi*, a root doctor who has strong supernatural abilities, the *omushakyizi*, and a spirit medium who can remove the witchcraft spirits from you. He is *omugirwa*."

"But what I have learned," I said, "is that there is a 'witch,'—called *mchawi*, and a 'healer'—the *mganga*. You're telling me there is a broader reality to witchcraft, there are more roles, more kinds of witches and witch-cleansers in some Bantu areas?"

Tsuma Washe, or Kajiwe (Little Stone) demonstrating in a witch-hunting ceremony, as he appeared in the Kenya press (1987).

* Later, in the 1970s and 1980s, Kajiwe was by far the most notorious witch-hunter in Kenya, working both on the coast and in central Kenya.

"Yes," she said. "It is much more complex than you said. There are many roles. You should learn the language of witchcraft. You should get a new teacher. Come to Kabale. My father will teach you. He is an *omushakyizi* and an *omumungi*—a good one, too—very smart, very respected."

I didn't dare tell her I was afraid to go to Kabale because that was where I had met a man with a crossbow...the man who thought *I* was a witch.

Charity Masembe closed her thesis and rested it on her lap. "Oh," she said, almost in a whisper. "Did you know there was a coup this morning?"

5

Witchcraft and Violence

1971–1978

Idi Amin Dada, Uganda dictator
Julius Kawawa, High Court Judge, Tabora, Tanzania
Ben Mpazi, Area Police Commander, Tabora, Tanzania

O n January 25, 1971, Colonel Idi Amin Dada of Uganda
seized power in what he claimed was a bloodless coup. Two
days later, with three others, I was able to interview him at
the Apollo Hotel swimming pool. At that point Amin was
a hero, a man whom many believed would put an end to the lawless
magendo (bandit) gangs in Kampala and to the rampant corruption in
the government. The exiled president, Milton Obote, was publicly vili-
fied. Idi Amin was seen as a savior.

Idi Amin addressing a public rally following his coup, Kampala, Uganda, 1971. (Author's photo)

The interview opened with great joviality, handshakes and smiles, Amin totally relaxed in his swimming trunks with a towel around his neck. He assured us that he needed our advice, that his concern for his people was genuine and that our governments (British, Dutch, American) would be his best friends—particularly if we gave him a good report from these interviews. The first questions were about his plans for the army (which still had many Obote supporters), his opinion of Uganda's rich Asians (the merchant class), what new appointments he might announce, and messages from other African presidents. Amin was evasive, and the more direct the question, the more evasive he became. Whenever he really did not like a question he would stand up, throw off his towel, dive into the pool, swim slowly in a circle, try to splash his guards, and come back to poolside to ask "Next question, please."

My first impression of Amin was of a rotund, jovial buffoon, effusive and self-congratulatory, and nothing I learned in that first meeting hinted at anything sinister. Nevertheless, within six months, dozens of organized murders made his regime an example of state-sponsored terrorism. Amin's lieutenants used widespread beliefs in witchcraft as a propaganda tool. Rumors were spread that the General drank the blood of his victims, sat with the bodies of his enemies and talked to their spirits. It was claimed that Amin had extraordinary powers of detection and witch-finding. Within the year, Amin's government increasingly played on witchcraft beliefs to bolster the state, and used witchcraft-based terror tactics to keep him in power.*

Later in 1971 I returned to Tabora in Tanzania to do research in the villages I had known in the mid-1960s. I found a room in the town at the old Railway Hotel, a run-down version of the lodge used in the 1890s by German colonial administrators and soldiers traveling inland. It was a rambling, one-story building with a garden and tall shade trees overlooking a patio bar.

On the first day I fell into conversation with another guest, a stocky, graying African in a dark suit and blue silk tie, curiously overdressed in this warm place. Julius Kawawa was the new Tanzanian High Court Judge for the region, staying at the hotel while his government house was repainted.

There were usually only five or six people at the hotel, and the judge and I often had tea or a beer together in the late afternoon. The third time we met I asked about his ideas on witchcraft. He loosened his necktie and eyed the last cucumber sandwich on the tea tray.

"Are you working for the government?" he asked.

"Oh no…No! " I stammered, shaken by the question.

"A government commission is coming to study the local witchcraft murders. I thought you might be a part of that business."

"No, I'm just interested," I said. "I am trying to understand how it works."

"I'll tell you what I can," the judge said. "First, I divide all witchcraft-related crimes into two types: the *spontaneous*, such as when a mob attacks a thief in a market, often because he is believed to be a witch, to have witchcraft powers to steal without being seen. Or there are the witchcraft accusations in bars, at funerals and most of the witchcraft-based crimes within a family.

"The other is *opportunistic,* killings for profit made to look like the attack of a witch, or a planned vigilante or secret society killing of a supposed witch, or the political violence you saw with Idi Amin. It's all planned. Manipulating people with fear of witchcraft at election times is another. Overall, however, I believe nearly half of the witchcraft crimes—both spontaneous and planned—occur within families." He reached for his pen and drew a half circle on the back of a hotel place-mat. I scrambled to copy it into my notebook, then pushed it back across to the judge.

"OK," he nodded, "but the 'for profit' section needs to be bigger in your drawing—it has a lot of activity. Protection against witchcraft can cause people to do a lot of awful things."

"Awful things?" I asked.

"Yes, killing for body parts or blood, even skin to dry and put into medicines, collecting dangerous plants, selling poisons—it's extraordinary what people will do for protection against witchcraft. A lot of peo-

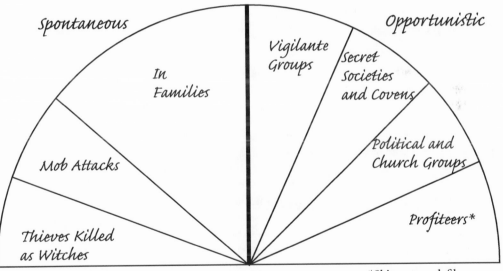

Categories of Witchcraft Violence

*Skin gangs, defilers, individual herbalists and witch finders

ple exploit witchcraft fears by selling concoctions. Healers push all sorts of things, protective medicines, good luck charms. Healers even suggest that people can protect themselves from witchcraft by child defilement."

"Child defilement and witchcraft?" I asked.

"Of course...many cases, particularly in Uganda."

The judge saw my confusion. "Look, a traditional healer takes money to protect a man from witchcraft or to cure his veneral disease. The healer gives him medicine and then says the treatment *also* calls for sex with a child or young adult. It's vicious, very bad...it leads to child abuse, often rape. Big problem in Uganda."

I filled in the judge's chart with "defilement" and we sat looking at it. Finally he ate the last cucumber sandwich, changed the subject to Tanzanian soccer for a moment, then stood to go. "Let's meet tomorrow around five," he said, scribbling in his appointment book. "I have someone for you to meet."*

The next afternoon I found the judge sitting with a uniformed policeman. I thought for a moment that I was in trouble, but when the officer saw me, he jumped up and began clapping.

"*Mwalimu, mwalimu!* (teacher, teacher)," he cried as he strode forward to shake hands. The judge was wide-eyed. The officer looked back

"Look, a traditional healer takes money to protect a man from witchcraft or to cure his HIV."

---

* Judge Kawawa's reference to thieves killed in markets as witches struck a chord with me because I had witnessed three such attacks on men caught stealing. One survived because police saved him, but two were stoned to death. Years later, in 2004, I had a fourth experience. On a sunny afternoon two teenage thieves were found in a women's dormitory just off the campus of Makerere University in Kampala and the alarm brought dozens of male students from their quarters next door.

One of the teenagers escaped, but the other was caught, stoned to death, and his body set on fire in front of the dorm. Students later reignited the fire for press photos. The explanation offered by many was that the thief who escaped did so through witchcraft. The incident alarmed the faculty at Makerere as a horrifying reminder of summary executions in the Amin era. Many students agreed with their teachers but some did not. One called it a "deterrent to others." Another said it was "vigilante justice...our basic right to economic survival."

at the judge. "He was my teacher in Dar es Salaam! This *mzungu* (European), he was my *mwalimu!* "

It was true. Six years before, at the new University of Dar es Salaam, I had worked with Ben Mpazi in a class of young government officers. Now I received the wonderful Tanzanian greeting between old friends: slapping hands, snapping fingers, amazement, wonder, "oohs," "ahs," big smiles.

After our course together, Ben had gone into the Tanzanian police and risen through the ranks. For the past year he had been the Tabora Area Police Commander. When he got over the surprise that we knew each other, Judge Kawawa came to the point.

"Mpazi, tell Norman what you think about *uchawi*. Maybe he can help with the commission. He knows the business."

Ben paused, and for the first time the smile faded from his face.

"Witchcraft is a big problem here, *mwalimu*. We are all struggling to cut down the cases. There is a lot of killing, mostly of elders, usually after droughts or floods. That's why a government commission is coming. They will ask a lot of hard questions. They could be very critical of me and my officers."

As we talked I began to understand the complexity of the violence. The killings were often preceded by a witchcraft accusation against the supposed witch, as in the case of Mohammadi. The kind of murders varied from ritual killings by a gang to mob killings of a suspected witch, or vigilante-style killings believed done for the good of the community. Another witchcraft-related crime was grave-robbing to obtain flesh or body parts for anti-witchcraft medicines. The judge also said that flesh-eating and ritualistic cannibalism were related to witchcraft beliefs and that he had seen several cases in court. As we talked, it became clear that one of the judge's concerns was the large number of violent witchcraft cases within families.

"It is not hard to understand," he said. "Remember, we have big, extended families who often live in one homestead—children, parents, grandparents, cousins, uncles, aunts. Some men have two or even three wives and of course there are a lot of witchcraft accusations among co-wives. Even the threat of witchcraft is a way to control people, a way to

Another witchcraft-related crime was grave-robbing to obtain flesh or body parts for anti-witchcraft medicines.

punish someone, a way to break intolerable relationships. One co-wife can try to chase another off the *shamba* (farm) by accusing her of *uchawi*. Witchcraft can be just a cover-up or an excuse for a violent attack."

As he talked it dawned on me that the chief's poison case in Usagari that I had seen earlier was such a case, where witchcraft is used as a cover-up or explanation of a murder.

"What we worry about in court is the victim," the judge continued, "and the effects witchcraft has on the local society. In serious cases the cost to even a suspected witch is terrible. A person's reputation can be shattered, their status reduced to that of an outcast. People can lose property, be beaten or fined by the local home guards and lose the right to be treated with traditional etiquette. The daughters of an accused witch can become unmarriageable, and all the children in the family stigmatized for life. Divorce may follow. If administrators or the police don't provide an external solution, the accused witch may be driven out of the village, even killed."

"I saw one of those cases in Usagari," I said. "A woman called Mohammadi."

The judge nodded. He looked down, then spoke quietly. "We weep for these people…there are so many who suffer from this business."

In a meeting later that week I showed the judge a list of secret societies that I had learned about over the years and asked him what he thought the connections to witchcraft might be. Talking to him I had realized that many such groups used witchcraft threats to carry out their work.

"Secret societies are very common," he said. "Sure, we judges know something since we see them in court. It depends which ones you are talking about.

"Quite a collection," the judge said, without looking up. "I know the ones in Tanzania. I think most of those Kenyan groups are really political fronts—the Mwakenya, like Mau Mau. The Kamba groups are to settle land disputes and hurt people who violate boundary agreements."

EAST AFRICAN SECRET SOCIETIES

Amyanbuda   Ritual killing gangs believed seeking human body parts. Wanji culture, Njombe area, Tanzania.

Chinza Chinza   Assassination and terror group, southwest Tanzania, night-stalking, throat-cutting.

Devil Cults   In Kenya, groups allegedly engaging in devil worship, satanic acts, sexual orgies, and cannibalism.

Lion-men   Cults using assassins disguised in lion skins, killing by slashing with lion claws, Tanzania. Similar to leopard cults in West Africa.

Mashala Gangs   Terror gangs, north-central Tanzania.

Mumani   Blood hunting cult, northern and central Tanzania, believed to involve ghosts. Possible selling of blood for ritual purposes.

Mwakenya   A secret political support group in central Kenya, mainly among Kikuyu people, occasionally using terror tactics and witchcraft threats for recruitment.

Othileo Groups   In Kenya, Kamba people's oathing groups, used for intimidation and election coercion, and historically for settlement of land disputes.

Rufiji Covens   Witchcraft groups in Tanzania's Rufiji river delta, demanding ritual killing as an initiation requirement.

Shetani Groups   Believers in spirits or *jinns*, occasionally violent groups, coastal areas of Tanzania and Kenya. May involve women's spirit possession cults.

Skin Gangs   Killing groups seeking body parts as commodities for trade, Mbeya Region, Tanzania.

Sungusungu   Original home-guard organizations in central Tanzania supported by government; some became secret and are believed to have engaged in assassination of suspected witches; promoted in other parts of Tanzania as self-help home guards.

Vaya   A secret society found mainly north of Mombasa on the coast of Kenya.

He kept studying the list, tapping his pencil on the desk.

"Of the Tanzanian groups, the Lion-men are gone...we have had a case or two...but gone. The Amyanbuda and Chinza Chinza... I worked in the south, in Mbeya. Those boys are sleeping too. They only get organized when there is money to be made. We had some cases where they were selling body parts."

He went on, giving me the status of the groups he knew, dismissing the Shetani cults as a bunch of women who conduct peaceful, self-protection ceremonies. "OK, these Rufiji covens—I suspect there are some still out there, but we have not had recent trouble. These Mumani Ghost groups...they are just fakes, intimidators."

"Is there a pattern?" I asked. "Do these secret societies have anything in common...a red thread?"

The judge kept looking at the list, now his head in his hands.

"You make me feel like I'm back in law school, looking for crime patterns. Maybe...sure, a few patterns. First, all these groups use *random* violence to establish their power. Kill an old lady, a child, someone on the way to the well. Nothing terrorizes a village like an unexplained killing. You need terror to sell protection. Sure, too, most of these groups rely on a belief in evil spirits, hidden devils, that nonsense. A lot use witchcraft indirectly, simply by suggesting it is around. That is what creates terror. They blame witchcraft, witchcraft is camouflage. A lot of these groups play with symbols—like a skull, an animal skin, maybe a gourd of medicines, a password, a secret handshake."

I started to tell him of the photo images I had collected about witchcraft, but at that point, maybe because he was getting tired, Kawawa became testy.

"This all makes Africans look damn primitive. What about your violent societies in America...what about your Mafia?" In one sentence he had turned the tables.

"That would be one," I stammered. "But there are others. The old Ku Klux Klan...do you remember them? They were a secret society."

"I do," he said. "They were gangs of white men who hung your blacks—lynched them...did night raids on horseback, wore white hoods and spread terror with symbols like burning crosses. Sure, we

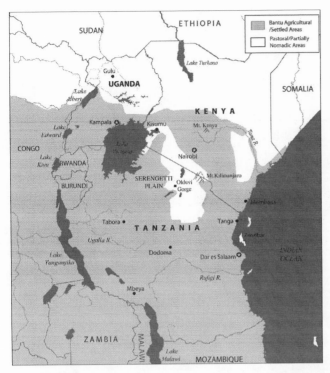

Bantu Areas: Pastoral vs. Agricultural Regions (Map by Ellen Kozak)

studied them in school. Your southerners hated blacks and called them 'niggers.' My instructor said the big reason was to protect white jobs."

I wanted to say that my family was from Vermont, that we didn't do those things, that it was a long time ago and that things were better now. Instead we sat in silence. On the wall behind the judge was a big map of East Africa and it gave me a chance to change the subject.

"Can we map where some of these secret societies are? Can we map the kinds of witchcraft in East Africa?" I said, pointing to the map. He gave me a vacant stare and I thought he would say no, but he got up and went to the big map.

"Why not? Let's try," he said, pointing with his pencil. "The Mumani are here, old Lion-men here, killing for body parts seems to be here and here. The *sungusungu* gangs here in the west, from Lake Victoria to Mbeya. Hell yes, you map these things. I'll help you. It could be very interesting."

That afternoon I went to a butcher shop, bought several big pieces of paper and spent the night drawing a rough map. When I brought it to Kawawa he studied it for a long time.

"A good beginning, but one big problem," he finally said. "You need to make a distinction between Bantu farm groups and the pastoralists like the Maasai. The pastoralists don't have these problems. Witchcraft ideas are in Bantu areas, among farmers—that's our big witchcraft zone. All across here...the Congo, southern Uganda, in western and central Kenya, particularly Kisii. And most of Tanzania, except Maasailand. And in both countries the coastal zones, lots of mixed Muslim and Bantu witchcraft ideas."

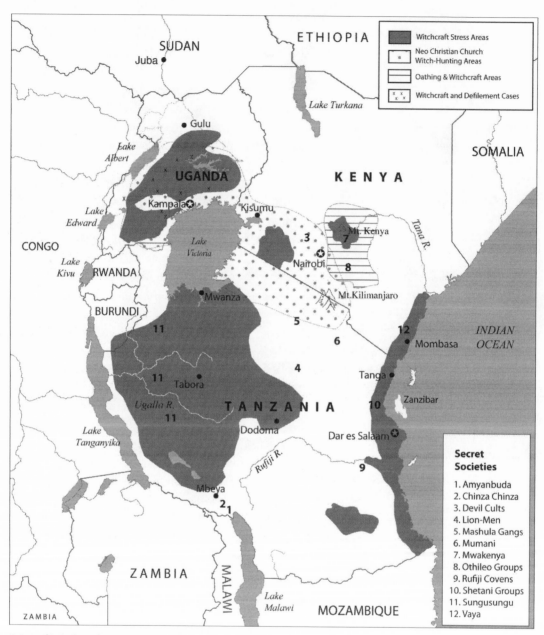

Map of Witchcraft Practices. Examples of how witchcraft beliefs are used in East Africa and examples of secret societies that use witchcraft threats and witch hunting. (Map by Ellen Kozak).

He paused and thought for a moment. "Draw it again. We will show it to Commander Mpazi. The police will be very interested in the extent of this stuff."

Because of our map discussions, Judge Kawawa apparently decided I needed a lesson in witchcraft law and, the next time we met, he launched into a diatribe against the Tanzanian witchcraft laws.

"You know our witchcraft ordinance comes from colonial times, from the South African anti-witchcraft laws of the 1890s, adopted here by the British. They didn't work then and they don't work today."

He ordered a Fanta soft drink and three cucumber sandwiches, then continued. "Look at the damn law! It is an offense for anyone to claim witchcraft powers, to possess 'instruments' of witchcraft, to supply paraphernalia or poisons for witchcraft practice, to give advice about witchcraft, to accuse anyone of being a witch or to solicit the services of a claimed witchcraft practitioner...all still in place."

"I don't understand the problem," I said as he pushed a sandwich to me.

"The laws are not African—they clash with African traditional laws. You know this. Africans have always hated witchcraft. The killing of a witch is often done with the agreement of the community. What's that mean?"

I tried to offer an answer, but he didn't wait.

"It means prosecuting a person who killed a 'witch' can be seen as very unfair by the people. We are prosecuting someone who did a 'community service.' Of course, the state, the court sees the event as murder, a crime against the state, a blow to civil order."

"In reality, two systems—I understand," I said. "I know about an African judge in Malawi, among the Yao people, who conducts all the witchcraft hearings outside his courtroom at a place under a shade tree. He wants to symbolize the difference between Western codes and traditional codes."

"Never get away with that up here," Kawawa said, eating the last sandwich and getting ready to leave. "The high court would have us sacked. Look, witchcraft has existed in Africa for thousands of years, and has always been hated. People believe themselves victimized by witches. Witches have been publicly executed, tortured, their property confiscated, always treated with contempt. How do we deal with these killings when they are believed to be in self-defense against a witch or for the public good? Witch-killers are sometimes seen as heroes. Anyway, visit the district courts...sit in on a witchcraft trial. You'll learn what we judges are up against."

I took the judge's advice and over the next few months sat in on five witchcraft trials, all in different settings. The lower courts on the Tanzania coast in Kisarawe District and in Mbeya town were in open-air buildings, onlookers standing outside the windows, chickens pecking around under the trees, vendors selling fruit and cigarettes. Inside, the atmosphere was usually hushed, the defendant in the dock, the magistrate in a black robe, a few uniformed police standing guard.

The cases I saw were long and tedious, the officials obviously bored, the defendants sullen and silent before the bench. There were, however, occasional clashes. In one, a man whose son was about to be tried for witchcraft was caught outside the judge's chambers blowing smoke through the window, trying to drug the judge. The man was brought before the same judge, charged with contempt of court and given three months in jail. In another witchcraft case, the defendant's uncle dumped blood on the floor, released birds and spread salt on the benches of the courtroom. After his arrest he said he acted to scare the witnesses and keep them from testifying against his nephew. He also got three months.

A case I did not see but heard about concerned a man's complaint in court that he had paid a witch to turn his wife into a crocodile. When the transformation failed, the husband sued the practitioner for breach of contract. This was in nearby Malawi where a new traditional court system was in place. The plaintiff won the case at the first level and, upon appeal, at the second. The case then went into the government court system for review and was thrown out as an "impossible contract."

⁙

Several months later when I returned to Tabora and stopped by Judge Kawawa's chambers, I first got a rousing welcome.

...a man whose son was about to be tried for witchcraft was caught outside the judge's chambers blowing smoke through the window, trying to drug the judge.

"Ah, the wandering *mzungu* (European)," he shouted as the clerk showed me into his chambers. "Very good to see you! How are you? How is the witchcraft project?"

"OK," I said. "How is Ben the policeman? Can we have a reunion?"

The judge lost his smile. He went to the door and ordered tea from the clerk, closed the door and returned to his desk.

"Sad news. Mpazi was demoted and transferred to Morogoro. It happened when that government commission came to investigate the witchcraft murders—four new killings occurred while they were here! Mpazi was blamed for bad police work and for not protecting people. He was sacked, demoted, then transferred. I think his career is over. Anyway, I will come to the hotel at five."

The judge believed the commission was very unfair to Mpazi and the entire district police force. "You know," he said, "in these huge districts witchcraft investigations are costly because there are never enough police, or vehicles with petrol. Even clear-cut cases can fall apart when the damn witnesses run away. I have seen it."

He became a little upset as he listed reasons witchcraft crimes are so hard to bring to trial. "In remote rural areas, victims are often buried secretly, without death reports. Even when crimes are reported, evidence can be hard to gather, and hearsay hard to distinguish from fact. In remote police posts, officers can be reluctant to get involved in a witchcraft case for fear of retaliation against their families. Even in court, there are a lot of claims of self-defense. You know, 'I was provoked,' or 'The witch attacked me,' or 'I killed him to save myself'."

I told Judge Kawawa that I had heard about police being intimidated in witchcraft cases since my first days in Africa, from the curator at Ft. Jesus in Mombasa. He nodded and then launched into a summary of his views on witchcraft in the broader society. I wrote notes as fast as I could.

"I see witchcraft as a hidden form of authority that frankly can supersede government laws. These beliefs are a closed, self-perpetuating way of thinking. They provide explanations for mysterious events, and explain calamities or untimely deaths. They are really a convoluted system of thought that allows responsibility for some unfortunate event to be transferred to any person who is already a social outcast, misfit, or damn deviant." He paused, then looked at me with a wry smile.

"It is also called scapegoating—I think it happens all over the world."

I wanted to ask him to speculate on why the government had failed to curtail the witchcraft violence, but he had something else to add and seemed to want to end the conversation.

"Look, my friend, you need to look into the new evangelical cults. Put them on the witchcraft map. These 'born agains' are spreading out of Uganda like, what do you say in your country? Yeah, like wildfires. Some of them are involved with witchcraft and they can cause a lot of conflict in their witch-hunting."

6

The Spirit Wars

1980–1986

Simon Sirkoi, member of religious sect, Kenya
David Barrett, missionary, scholar, Nairobi, Kenya
Jasper Holyoak, former missionary, Kenya coast
Paul Baxter, anthropologist, northern Kenya
Wako Diriba, nomadic leader, the Boran, Kenya
Peter Boru, teacher, northern Kenya
Christine X, patient, Makerere Hospital, Uganda
Nathan Chisholm, Alabama missionary, Tanzania

In the fall of 1980 while changing a flat tire on the Kenya-Uganda border, I learned something about "Christian witchcraft." Sweating, dirty and tired, I had just washed my hands from the four-gallon *debe* of water on the front of the Land Rover when a procession of marchers came into view. Most were singing or blowing small horns or whistles and a few carried white flags with crosses sewn on them Most of the children were barefoot. When they turned off the road to gather under a shade tree I moved the Mzee to be closer, got out and sat on the fender to watch. After the final prayer one of the congregation came to greet me.

"Welcome, brother," he said. "You can see us again next Saturday. We will march here again...yeah, right here."

"Thank you," I said, standing to shake his hand. "But I will be in Kampala. Maybe on the way back."

His name was Simon Sirkoi, a tall, lanky teacher with a blue cross sewn on his white robe. He looked about thirty. After establishing who I was and who he was, I apologized for asking a direct question.

Evangelist preachers address a crowd of communicants in a type of outdoor ceremony found throughout East and central Africa (Umatli, Zimbabwe, 1966).

"How does your group view witchcraft?"

He smiled and looked right at me. "Ah yes, brother, that is our 'spirit war.'"

Simon Sirkoi compared a witch to Satan, a coven of human witches to a pack of devils. He said his sect was an offshoot of an older movement known as Dini ya Msambwa—the Creed of the Cross—and they believed deeply that witchcraft was the scourge of all society. It was the obligation of everyone to ferret out witches. He looked straight at me.

"We want to find them in our villages, to bring them in, to cleanse them and convert them to our movement."

"You use witch-hunting to recruit sect members?" I asked.

He thought for a moment. "Yes, for sure. We have three duties. First to find witches and bring them to our faith, then make them repent, then convert them."

Simon Sirkoi alerted me to how witchcraft is treated by East Africa's religious sects. To learn more I talked to David Barrett, a missionary–scholar based in Nairobi who earlier had published an excellent book on the "breakaway" church movements, *Schism and Renewal in Africa: An Analysis of Six Thousand Contemporary Religious Movements*. He defined a sect as a movement with a name, a leader, a location and a large enough following to be registered with the local government. Many of the six thousand groups he talked about were led by a self-proclaimed prophet and only flourished for a short time, then faded into obscurity.

Many prophets or sect leaders claimed to be able to identify witches and used these powers to build their movements. Some believed Satan was behind the power of witchcraft while others suggested that witchcraft was carried out by covens or devil cults. Anyone opposed to the sect was considered a witch and, as in Simon Sirkoi's group, it was the duty of a member to find witches and bring them into the movement.*

* David Barrett taught me to see East Africa as a religious mosaic, first divided into Christian, Muslim and traditional religions, and then into hundreds of different groups. Many were messianic or millennial sects that had broken away from a mainline church. Still others were what Barrett called "nativistic," that is groups that combined traditional ideas such as ancestor worship, female circumcision, traditional manners and dress with some dogmas from Christianity. Both the nativistic movements and the separatist Christian churches were usually led by self-proclaimed prophets. Many wrote their own doctrines and composed their own hymns. Some claimed that Jesus was racially black, or described the 12 apostles as pure African with African names and traits. Others promoted drumming and chanting in church, used secret emblems, special handshakes and wore distinctive garb, often white robes. Some of the groups that survived evolved into the new evangelical or "born again" churches.

Soon after my meeting with David Barrett, a momentous event occurred. Judith von Daler, the pretty lady I had met in New York at the Museum of Modern Art, became Judith von D. Miller. The civil ceremony, with three friends in attendance, was held at the Nairobi Provincial Commissioner's office, the license registered and immortalized at the US Embassy.

After the wedding we moved to a place called Ukunda on the south Kenya coast, Judy to write a book on African art and I to finish a proposal for a new departure—educational filmmaking. We lived on the edge of a rainforest, right on the sea in a house built of coral block and grass thatch. Although probably unnecessary, wooden poles had been tied between the top of the walls and the roof thatch to keep leopards out. There was no electricity, no running water, and only a hand-filled tank provided showers behind the house. In front, there was a lone baobab tree overlooking the sea and, on moonless nights, hyenas occasionally could be seen scooping crayfish from the tidal pools below.

Author and wife, near Ukunda village, south coast of Kenya. Beach house, baobab tree and cliffs (opposite page) believed by local fishermen to be sacred for ritual healing and the cleansing of witchcraft. (Author's collection)

On occasion groups of people came to the cliffs, to a place below the baobab tree for spirit cleansing rituals. As I had learned from Kabwere Wangi on the north coast some years before, in local Digo culture some illnesses were believed caused by spirits, others by witches. Most of the rituals were witchcraft-cleansings.

Before sunset one evening, a procession of twelve people walked slowly down the beach behind two men who carried a woman in a wooden chair. She was wrapped in bright *kikois* with a scarf around her neck and flowers in her hair. The group stopped at water's edge below the cliff near our house facing the sea. As a drum beat and people clapped, the two men carried the woman into the water up to their waists. She was tipped back, lowered and submerged for a few moments. This happened three times while women on the shore threw back their heads to trill.

When the men came out of the water, they put the sick person gently on the sand and started a fire, fanning the smoke away with banana fronds. One big woman rubbed her with oil as others dried her with towels and wrapped her in dry *kikois*. Most were singing in unison. Two men passed small cakes and flowers and, in perhaps thirty minutes, the procession started back down the beach, this time the ill woman slowly walking as others sang.

(Cliff painting by Judy Miller)

A few days later we described the scene to Jasper Holyoak, a retired European missionary who lived four miles up the beach. "My God," he exclaimed. "You could have been killed instantly! They are practicing witchcraft! If they had seen you they would have attacked with their *pangas*. You could have been cut to pieces. You made a terrible mistake going near."

Judy had always thought Jasper Holyoak exaggerated what little he knew about African culture, despite his thirty years in Kenya. The next day Judy talked to Saidi, an old fisherman who came to our door with fresh fish almost daily. She asked what danger we faced.

"None, mama, none," Saidi said with a broad grin. "Those people are from my village. They told me they had come here because of the spirits in the rocks below the tree. They were cleansing their sister of witchcraft. Oh yes, they saw you. They wanted to offer you cake, but you didn't come near." When Saidi left our house, Judy looked at me with a smile.

"On your witchcraft ideas...yet another way these beliefs can be misunderstood, this time by narrow-minded white folks!"

A month later, somewhat to our surprise, we did receive a grant to make educational films. The topic was how people adapt to different environments around the world.* The northern desert of Kenya was to be the first location. We planned to live with a pastoral group called the Boran, who historically survived on milk from their herds. It took several months to get the equipment and hire a film crew but finally we set up our tents on the edge of a mission station in Marsabit, a district outpost in the old Northern Frontier District.

Some Boran had settled around Marsabit town and were growing maize, but others continued to follow their herds. We decided to film both lifestyles and try to understand the transition between a pastoralist and an agricultural way of life. Beliefs in evil eye and witchcraft were of special interest to me. The cultural adviser to the project was a British anthropologist, Paul Baxter, who had lived with the Boran and written about their beliefs. One night, around the campfire, I asked him if it were true that pastoralists didn't practice witchcraft.

"It depends how much a group mixes herding with agriculture," he said. "The greater the reliance on agriculture and settlement in one place, the greater the chance you'll find witchcraft accusations."

"More herding, less witchcraft?" I asked.

He wagged his head in vague agreement, and went on. "When Boran do make witchcraft accusations, it is usually against new migrants into their areas, or against people of other ethnic groups. Boran on the

* The project, supported by the National Science Foundation, was to produce films and develop teaching materials for college-level courses. The locations we eventually visited were in Afghanistan, Bolivia, two parts of China and Kenya, each chosen to illustrate different ecological zones and different ways of human adaptation in mountains, high plateaus, deserts, coastal zones and islands. The series was entitled "The Faces of Change."

move don't bother with witchcraft. Sure, they believe in the evil eye, but evil eye only creates minor ailments."

As the film-making progressed, an elder named Wako Diriba, the leader of one of the nomadic groups, became a spokesman about Boran culture. It was in his remote cattle camp, with Baxter's help, that I asked the old man about witchcraft and evil eye.

"Witchcraft? Witchcraft is not for a true Boran," Wako said, looking disgusted. "People who follow the herds don't believe those things. Only Boran who settle and become farmers use it. Those Boran near Marsabit town who grow maize, they are not true Boran, they do not live by cattle. They use witchcraft on themselves. Even on others."

While Baxter was asking another question, Wako eyed me carefully then began spitting on the ground. "It doesn't mean anything," Baxter whispered. "He is not hostile. It is an elder's habit."

"Good," I said trying to smile at Wako. "What about evil eye?"

The two fell into a long, animated conversation, Wako spitting three more times. Finally, Baxter turned to me.

"He says evil eye does exist among Boran and other pastoralists around here: Gabbra, Rendille, even Turkana. He calls them 'eyers,' people who can harm people. He says they are the poor, and only keep sheep and goats. They are men without cattle. He considers them rubbish and calls them 'bush creatures.' He says they screw their sheep."

Baxter gave me a glance that said "Let's not pursue the sheep screwing bit."

"How do 'eyers' work? What happens to the victims?" I asked.

There was another conversation in Boran. Then Baxter spoke again.

"'Eyers' are people who stare at someone for an overly long time, people with strange eyes, red eyes, or a crossed eye. It is believed they can cause illness or bad luck—minor things like scabies, rashes, cuts on the feet. They can make people listless, cause a loss of appetite. And they are particularly dangerous for children and babies. Mothers keep toddlers away and cover children when 'eyers' are around."

"Sounds like 'eyers' are scapegoats," I said. "The lower rungs on the ladder: outcasts, someone to blame. Just like witches."

"Of course," Baxter said, as if everyone in the world knew this except

Wako Diriba, nomadic group leader.

Peter Boru and Wako Diriba with film booklets. (Author's collection)

me. "Also, Wako wants you to understand that true Boran who live with their herds do not have witchcraft. He is concerned you understand this."

Thanks to Wako and Baxter, the lesson from the desert I gained was that as long as people were mobile, there were no witchcraft accusations. Evil eye, yes, witchcraft, no. It was when pastoralists settled and began lifestyles that brought them into close contact with others that witchcraft accusations crept onto the scene. Anthropologists speculate that the denser and more hierarchical societies made possible by agriculture lead to conflict and the need for a system of controlling power. Witchcraft filled this role. I remembered my trek in the eastern Congo with the Ituri pygmies where Jean Pierre Hallet had taught me that pygmies were witch-free until they settled and went to work for Bantu farmers on the edge of the forest. I also vaguely remembered that James Kirkman at Ft. Jesus had said that neither nomadic pastoralists nor hunter/gatherers, like the pygmies, had witchcraft until they began to grow food and settle in villages. Kirkman had speculated that the first human settlement in Africa was about 9000 BC, and that witchcraft probably began then.

Seven years after filming in Northern Kenya I was finally able to take the films back and arrange a showing at the local school. Aside from Wako Diriba, another key individual in the films had been a 14-year-old lad named Peter Boru. When I returned he had become a primary school teacher in the town. We had published teaching guides to go with the films and both Wako and Peter Boru were featured on the covers. I wanted to give them both copies of the booklets. With Peter's help we found Wako Diriba in a remote cattle camp, fourteen miles from Marsabit town.

To get into the camp we had to descend a rocky trail and I could see Wako watching us climb down the trail. Peter went ahead, and after a formal greeting, they shook hands and spoke at length. Wako eyed me and a very slight smile came across his face. He spoke again in a hushed tone. Peter looked bewildered and motioned me closer.

"He says that they still have no witches here. They are true Boran—who follow herds. They don't believe in witches."

It had been seven years.

On the same trip to East Africa I was able to stop at Makerere in Uganda and meet James Mulira, a historian I had been in touch with who was studying the new born-again movement. I hoped to learn something more about how these religious groups dealt with witchcraft. And as we sat in his office that overlooked the tree-lined campus, he had a lot to say.

"Sure, there are many witchcraft issues in these born-again churches," he said, "partly because we have had such an upsurge in evangelical movement in the country. Some are legitimate, some get help from churches in America, from places like Akron, Ohio, but a lot are frauds. They are sects that play on fears of witchcraft to extort money. Their trick is to accuse someone, to offer salvation, and then exact a price for it."

Mulira said that a phenomenon new in East Africa since the 1970s is the "charismatic" churches that preach born-again, evangelical doctrines. Thousands have evolved, each from a tiny nucleus of people with a charismatic leader. Such leaders, often self-proclaimed prophets, see accused witches as arch sinners, and preach about them as satanic people. Like the early prophet movement described by David Barrett, the techniques used in the churches include constant praying, readings, singing, drumming, chants and incantations. Confessions are encouraged, often demanded, and then treated as revelations.

I told him about the Dini wa Shambwa movement on the Kenya border.

"Sure, that one is an old movement, but some of our groups do the same thing. Witchcraft is seen as the arch evil. It's old Calvinism, a punishing God who burns sinners and witches in hell. There is even a darker side to some of these new movements. In fact I have a colleague, a psychiatrist, who has a case that involves witchcraft, a patient who may have been tortured after she joined a sect to cure herself. She believed herself bewitched."

He thought for a moment. "Let me call Segge."

Dr. Seggane Musisi not only agreed to see me on short notice, but he brought two graduate students who were studying the psychology of religious extremism. We talked long into the afternoon and agreed to meet in a few days time, when the students returned from a field study in Mbarara. The next morning, however, as I sipped coffee at the Makerere guest house, one of the waiters dropped a note at my table. It was from Musisi. He was sending over the woman Professor Mulira had mentioned, since we had talked about the case in our seminar. Would I talk to her and try to help her? She had been his patient for nearly two years. The waiter nodded toward the lobby.

Dr. Musisi apparently thought I could help this woman by simply listening, a situation that made me uneasy since I had no qualifications to talk to psychiatric patients, even an outpatient. Nevertheless, I gulped the coffee and hurried to the lobby.

Her name was Christine, a 32-year-old woman with a year of university training, the wife of a police inspector and mother of two young children. All four family members were there. She was breast-feeding a baby and the father held a sleeping toddler. Christine thanked me for talking to her and came right to the point. She had joined a born-

"…sect members ministered to her with medicines, massage, prayers and constant chants of "Power to God."

again sect in Kampala to cure an illness that she described as constant stomach pain, backache, occasional vomiting, bulging eyes, trembling and periodic dizziness. She was articulate and talked earnestly as the baby fed.

She said the sect leader, a man named Obidiaha, claimed to be a healer. He insisted she spend two weeks in their compound where sect members ministered to her with medicines, massage, prayers and constant chants of "Power to God." When she asked to leave the compound the gates were locked, she was restrained and her legs tied. When she finally did escape and returned home, she told her husband the evangelist leader had tried to rape her and showed him rope burns on her legs.

Her husband nodded and added that the two weeks had cost a great deal of money. He looked bitter and said he believed many of the new charismatic churches were in the extortion business. Physical coercion and sexual abuse could be part of the mix. I listened and tried to look sympathetic, but something told me I could do more harm than good. Christine was obviously frustrated with my responses.

"Please," she said. "I have been like this for nearly two years. I must know if I am medically sick or spiritually sick—if I am bewitched."

The baby had stopped nursing and her husband took it from her.

"Christine," I said, "I think Dr. Musisi sent you here to be my teacher. You are teaching me about these churches. I don't know what is making you sick...I'm not that kind of doctor. I would encourage you to follow Dr. Musisi's advice. These things take time. He is highly respected."

She wanted to ask another question, but her two children had had enough. One began screaming and the other crawled off across the parquet floor into the kitchen. She shook her head, went to the door and called a nanny who had apparently been waiting outside. Christine took the car keys from her husband and gave the screaming child to the nanny, picked up the floor runner, thanked me, curtseyed in the old fashioned Ugandan way and left. It was, I suspect, part of their plan that the husband would stay for another word.

"Christine actually got sick just before our marriage—before we eloped," the Inspector said. "My family did not want me to marry her.

"I must know if I am medically sick or spiritually sick—if I am bewitched."

Could that be bothering her? Could my work as a policeman bother her? My work is on HIV/AIDS?"

"What's the work?" I said.

"I do HIV/AIDS education. Uganda police are like our military, they can have many partners and also sometimes take the virus home to their wives. Christine hears me talking about these problems all the time."

"Let me get this straight," I said. "You are a policeman, some policemen in Uganda, as elsewhere in the world, infect their wives, the wives have no power to demand condoms or protect themselves. On top of this Christine is not accepted by your mother, which must be hard for both of you."

He nodded.

"I think you are onto some of her problems, Inspector," I said. "Have you shared this information with Dr. Musisi?"

He shook his head no.

"I would," I said. "I think the two issues may be bothering her very much. I would definitely talk to Dr. Musisi."

He nodded several times and began to smile. "Yes, I will. And I will keep talking to my mother to accept her. I will make Christine believe she is safe. I will use condoms! I will tell her you said she is *not* bewitched, and that the born-again church that treated her was very bad."

I started to protest but he was already waving and half-way to the car.

"Come back soon," he shouted. "She will be better for sure. Come see us. Christine will cook chicken!"

Christine was a woman apparently victimized by Christian evangelical witch-hunters but in Tabora I met an American evangelist who didn't believe a Christian group could do such things. At the Railway Hotel I fell into a discussion with a young missionary, Nathan Chisholm from Mobile, Alabama. He had been in Africa for six weeks, proselytizing among the local Nyamwezi. The longer we talked the more tense the conversation became.

"I want to spread the news of Jesus," he said. "To build village churches, to bring them to Christ, to give them a new life."

"Who are 'them'?" I asked.

"Oh, all the locals, any non-Christians, anyone who will hear the glorious news. My wife and I work through prayers, we tell Bible stories, the words of the prophet Jesus, the words of God."

"They have already heard about God," I said. "Missionaries have been here for 150 years. David Livingston lived here for a while. He was a missionary, you know, trying to stamp out the slave caravans."

He looked confused.

"And the Catholics," I continued, "they have been here over a hundred years—Methodists, Lutherans, Pentecostals—a long time, none of them has solved the big problem yet."

"What's that?" he asked with a hint of annoyance.

"Beliefs in witchcraft. Witchcraft ideas lead to accusations against innocent people, violence, killing, banishing people as witches. I know a case just down the road. A woman called Mohammadi. Your Christian messages have not helped much. Why? Because most people around here use two or three systems of thought. They mix and match—a little Christianity, a little Islamic thought, traditional witchcraft ideas—whatever gets them through the day."

"When people hear the words of Jesus, they will turn away from witchcraft," Chisholm said.

"They *have* heard the words of Jesus and they don't turn away," I replied. "They really do hold witchcraft beliefs alongside Christian ideas. People look for explanations anyplace they can find them."

Chisholm became petulant. "Why, why?" he asked. "Why haven't Christians ended witchcraft?"

"Look," I said. "In some ways the Christian church has encouraged witchcraft. The mainline churches rail against it, thus giving it credibility. The independent churches conduct witch-hunts, the prophet sects use witchcraft eradication as a way to recruit members. Believe me, witchcraft beliefs are a part of the religious fabric around here. If it is any comfort to you, Islam doesn't have much luck either. Their clerics just ignore it. In fact they allow it as a parallel system."

He shook his finger, then slid forward in his chair as if he was going down on one knee to pray. "Not so," he exclaimed, "when the people

"Witchcraft ideas lead to accusations against innocent people, killing, banishing people as witches… Your Christian messages have not helped much."

hear the voice of Jesus...not so when they learn of God's will."

"Look, do you really want to know why Christians fail to stop witchcraft practices or not?" I asked.

He nodded and to my relief sat back in his chair.

"Christians, African leaders, white missionaries, generally preach to Africans that witchcraft does not exist, that it is impossible to do those things—that there are no such things as witches, magical powers, hyenas that fly in the night. At the same time the missionaries preach that there is a Satan, that Jesus walked on water, that Jesus was born of a virgin, rose bodily to a heaven up in the sky and that there is a Christian spirit world and some kind of holy ghost, just not an African spirit world."

"Those are Christian beliefs," he nodded.

"Christians can't confront witchcraft because their basic beliefs and witchcraft beliefs are based on the same things, on spirits, invisible agents, ghosts, magic, miracles. A Christian Satan or an African sorcerer is the same thing. A witch or a Christian devil, the same thing. And the blood and body of Christ, those sacraments are very hard to explain to potential African converts."

"Why?" Chisholm asked.

"Christians can't confront witchcraft because their basic beliefs and witchcraft beliefs are based on the same things…on spirits…"

"Think about it," I said. "You're telling a young African that this wafer is the body of Christ and this wine is his blood—while his or her parents have said that the worst crimes are to drink blood, eat human flesh, commit cannibalism. It's very confusing."

We sat in silence for several moments. "OK," he finally said. "What would you have us missionaries do about witchcraft? Give up? Accept it?"

"In my book," I said, "pushing your heavy-duty evangelical message, telling people how to believe and what to believe is wrong. If you want to build schools, dig wells, teach agriculture, set examples of fairness and justice, love and family, that's great. But pushing your brand of godliness down African throats? That is not so great. Witchcraft has to be confronted with education."

"You're anti-missionary?" he stammered.

"No, I'm ambivalent about missionaries, and, true, a little conflicted about your messages. Strange as it may seem to you, some of the missionaries from the southern United States are petty racists. They talk about Africans as 'them' and 'they,' and don't let Africans into their compounds without ringing a bell and waiting in the sun. They treat Africans like children. Do you know about 'posho-Christians'?"

He shook his head no.

"'Posho' means maize-meal. Some people turn Christian during drought seasons because a lot of missionaries will not give out food to non-Christians, without a commitment to the church. Also Africans can be critical for other reasons. A lot of mission stations have commandeered tracts of land and held them in the face of huge land shortages. Some of the more powerful missionary groups have meddled in the politics of the country, pushing their agendas."

"You don't sound conflicted, you sound...."

"I know, anti-missionary," I said. "It is not that simple."

I thought about my friend, Father Tablino, a Catholic priest living in a sweltering tin shack on the northern desert with the Boran herdsmen, providing medicines and teaching, and assuring me that if he converts one soul, his life in Africa will have been worth it. I thought of Stephen Houghton, now buried on Marsabit hill, the Anglican missionary who drove alone 340 miles to Nairobi to get famine food for the hungry huddled at his mission. That's the same man who bought medicines with his last personal money and drove back at night over bandit-infested roads that were occasionally mined by Somali.

"No," I said. "As long as you teach and bring relief to the poor, I'm pro-missionary. It's when you start forcing a particular rigid doctrine on Africans, that we part ways."

At that point a shiny new Ford Explorer pulled into the parking lot, and Chisholm's very pregnant wife and four children came to find him. "We are six workers for God," Chisholm smiled as he introduced Bonnie Jean Chisholm.

"Almost seven, sir," she drawled, patting her stomach. She then curtseyed like an old-fashioned southern girl, like the student at Makerere a few weeks earlier.

"Nice to meet you," I said. "Second time recently I have seen a pretty lady curtsey to me."

"Oh, I only do it to elders," she smiled.

7

Witchcraft and Juju Economics

1995

George Kuchar, salvage diver
Gilbert Olonana, ex-policeman, smuggler
Solostus Kasubi, physics teacher, Tabora, Tanzania
Saidi and Jaffa Mirisho, Tanzanian healers
Bismark Mwansasu, teacher, Tanzania
James Rweyemamu, Tanzanian researcher
Jonathan Ake, Nigerian, World Bank consultant

B y the 1990s a common government refrain in East Africa was that poverty lay behind witchcraft beliefs and that, in turn, witchcraft caused economic stagnation and slowed national development. I learned a lot about these murky economic processes from a salvage diver, a smuggler and a modern healer. Another friend, a World Bank consultant referred to the trade and trafficing of witchcraft objects as part of "juju economics."

At a beach bar near Konduchi, north of Dar es Salaam, I watched an unkempt European sailor bring a small boat into the cove, drop two anchors and lock the cabin. He put a bundle of cloths on his head and waded ashore through four feet of water.

"She'll ride OK. Two hooks out," he said to no one in particular as he stepped onto the veranda. He dropped his bundle of cloths on the floor, then went behind the bar, pushed glasses away from the sink and began to splash sand out of his hair. He was a salvage diver named George Kuchar, who worked on the wreck of the *Konigsberg*, the World War I German cruiser sunk in the Rufiji river 90 miles to the south. His sailboat carried a load of copper pipe.

He was in his mid-thirties, of medium height and walked with a limp that came from childhood polio. His parents were Polish and he was born on their sisal estate, near Tanga, north of Dar es Salaam. He described himself as an "uneducated Polak" who had married "above my rank" into a white settler family from Kenya.

"My wife died in childbirth," he said without emotion. "But the twins survived. Her parents blamed me for not taking her to Nairobi hospital. They took the boys through the Kenya courts. Real bastards, those people. They never liked me, never liked Poles."

"When was that?" I asked.

"Five years....maybe six. I lose track. I try to see the boys every year.... I think they are still five."

There was a long silence.

"What's the salvage routine?" I asked.

He brightened, apparently relieved to change the subject.

"Simple enough. I go under with a hard hat in an old diving suit. I have an African who pumps air down to me. I break off copper pipe, pull out portholes, bring up anything I can sell. When there is a load, I sail up here and get screwed by old Khan and his salvage yard. On the river I sleep on the boat, on the sails, under a net. I dive for lobster and spear fish and put out fish traps. We live on rice, fish and coconuts."

"Crocs?" I asked.

"Slimy bastards are around, but I'm not bothered. Maybe the bubbles frighten them, maybe the hard hat. Salimu has a rifle."

"Tell me about him," I said.

"Salimu? Ordinary wog. I pay him well and he keeps pumping when I'm under the water. He sleeps and gets laid a little way up-river where his *bibi* cooks for him. He has a family in Utete town. Actually he's a good bloke. We have a bond. As much as you can with a wog."

George waited, I think expecting a comment about calling Africans "wogs." I let it go. We sat there in silence.

"I could use help sailing back," he said casually. "It's a beautiful trip. Nobody out there except the odd smuggler. I can drop you on Mafia Island for your transport back...five days. You'll need a blanket, some rice and a few tins of food if fishing is bad."

We were gazing out at the shimmering ocean, his sailboat bobbing gently on the swells.

"OK," I said, without thinking. "Where? What time?"

He looked surprised, then broke into a broad smile.

"Great...that's great! Here, midnight, tomorrow midnight. We sail on the tide."

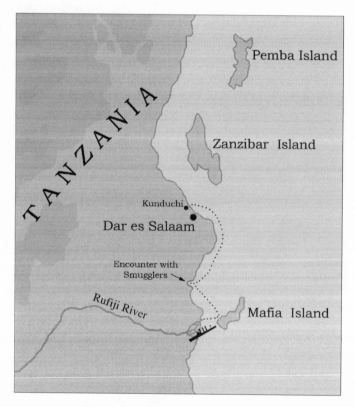

A sketch map of the author's route on the East African coast between Kunduchi and the Rufiji river delta, showing the site of the sunken German cruiser, Konigsberg. (Map by Peter C. Allen)

Three days later, just before sunset, eighty miles down the Tanzanian coast, we glided slowly around a headland of green mangrove trees and turned to anchor in a secluded harbor.

"Oh my Jesus," George whispered as we approached a wooden dhow with three men loading mangrove poles and oil cans. "Put your hands up...say 'salaama, salaama, peace, peace.' They are god-damn smugglers! They may think we're police."

Within seconds two Africans and an Arab had ducked below deck. The Africans came up with rifles, squatted at the rail and trained their guns on us. The Arab held onto the mast, a pistol in his other hand.

As we glided just twenty feet in front of them, George stood up with his hands in the air, an easy target.

"*Warafiki*...friends. No polici...no polici!"

Their guns followed us. George was motionless, his hands held high. I thought of the man with the cross-bow years ago in Uganda. We seemed not to be moving at all.

"George,...will we make it?" I whispered, squatting low in the boat.

"I think so...they don't want to deal with a murder case. The Arab may know me.... But stand up! Stand up, god-damn it! Put your hands up!"

At that moment our sail caught wind and we glided faster across the inlet. We pretended not to look at them and dropped anchor as far away as we could. I made a fire on the beach and George began diving for lobster. Just after sunset, there was a thump, thump of an engine and a tiny green light headed out to sea.

"What are they smuggling?" I asked.

"From here? Anything, everything. The mangrove poles are legal, but underneath the poles...who knows? Those oil drums probably have compartments for contraband—drugs, guns, ammunition, poisons, juju stuff...whatever this region has that's valuable up north, or for shipment inland, across Africa."

"Juju? What juju stuff?" I asked. "You know my interest in witchcraft, right?"

"Amulets, fetishes, dried monkey paws, body parts, poisons. They make amazing poisons around here. Salimu knows a lot. They can mix animal parts, battery acid, pesticides, plants, roots, other stuff. Amazing poisons."

"Does Salimu talk about witchcraft?" I asked.

"Yeah, sure. Sometimes. This Rufiji delta is famous for *uchawi* murders, usually carried out by covens of women. There were a lot of cases here in the 1960s. The government hung eight women—maybe more. They were in covens. Plenty of stories about witchcraft-related killing for human body parts, and making medicines, and selling the stuff inland—even as far as the Congo."

"Congo? How do they move it there?" I asked.

"The long-distance trade? Easy for small stuff—a lot goes on oil trucks, in those drums you saw near the dhow."

"Border inspections? Customs, searches?" I asked.

"OK, I'll tell you what I know. Long-haul lorries can carry two or three stacks of those oil drums–the 40-gallon cans. Some cans have hidden compartments, walled off from the oil. They are built so that when a border inspector puts a long stick into the container, he hits oil all the way down." He drew a sketch with his finger on the rolled-up sail. "All kinds of stuff can be smuggled in the empty part of the drum."

George had wrapped himself in a faded yellow *kikoi* and was about to stretch out on top of the sails. I had the place in the cabin.

"Ever try to move some of that stuff yourself?" I asked.

It was a dumb question, and I immediately wished I hadn't asked it. Just for a moment a shadow crossed George's face.

"This Rufiji delta is famous for uchawi murders, usually carried out by covens of women."

Salvage diver George Kuchar's sketches of how smugglers conceal contraband on small dhows and how a large oil drum may be divided to conceal goods next to a section containing oil.

George Kuchar and his sailboat off the coast of Tanzania. (Author's collection)

"Oh no…oh no," he said with conviction. "Those guys, the Arabs, they have a monopoly. I never smuggle anything."

I liked George Kuchar, sailor and salvage diver, but as I fell asleep I realized that I didn't believe him.

The trip with George Kuchar alerted me to the smuggling of witch-craft products, and on my next trips to East Africa I tried to interview people who dealt with the business—traders, herbalists, market people, local police or border officials. Usually I hit a stone wall, but finally on the slopes of Mt. Kilimanjaro, I found someone who knew smuggling and was willing to talk. Gilbert Olonana was a retired policeman and border guard, a man in his late forties whose mother was a Tanzanian Chagga and father a Maasai from the Kenya side of the mountain. I met Gilbert through his wife, Bernadetta, a faith healer whom I interviewed near Marangu village on the mountain.

"OK," he said, looking at my wrinkled map of East Africa. "I was a border guard in Kenya and later did a little of the business on my own—with donkeys. Just here, around Arusha."

He then bent closer to the map and began to peck on a place to the north, in central Kenya.

"First, for witchcraft things, a lot comes from Tharaka, here, by Mt. Kenya, on the lower slopes—a lot of dangerous roots and herbs and poisons, some made from horns and animal bones. The Tharaka healers are very feared. That's a botanical center for Kenya. At our border here, things like Firestone tires come south on donkeys, from Kenya."

"Donkeys? Tires?" I asked.

"Sure...it's a good trick. The donkeys are fed and watered on this side of the border in Tanzania, then taken across to graze. Over there, the smugglers load them with Kenya-made tires, and with medicines, transistor radios and witchcraft things, then turn them free. The donkeys wander back across the border to where they are fed and watered. They come home. No one gets caught because no one is with them. If the guards hear something and shoot into the night, they kill a donkey...that's all."

He pointed north of Nairobi again, to Mt. Kenya, and then drew a line with his finger south around Nairobi and across Maasailand to Mt. Kilimanjaro, then laid out other smuggling routes. From the Kenya coast inland to Kambaland, around Machakos was another route, or through Nairobi, sometimes on the rail line, then west toward Uganda. Zanzibar, also a botanical wonderland, was the source for all sorts of herbal concoctions used in rituals, some for witchcraft protection. Some items are moved on old slave routes toward the Congo, and from Tabora north to Lake Victoria. Some of the old routes go through the Usambara mountains near the coast, then to the west.

Earlier I had learned that both southwestern Tanzania, around Mbeya, and southwestern Uganda, around Kabale (where I had met the man with the cross-bow), were regions of heavy cross-border smuggling. Witchcraft items were part of shipments that included HIV medicines, drugs, bhang, cell phones, pocket radios and computers. The coffee smuggling routes between the Congo and north-central Uganda had been known for decades and often carried "juju things."

"Don't try it yourself," Gilbert warned. "Those boys are very jealous of their business. They will shoot in the night. They will treat you like a donkey."

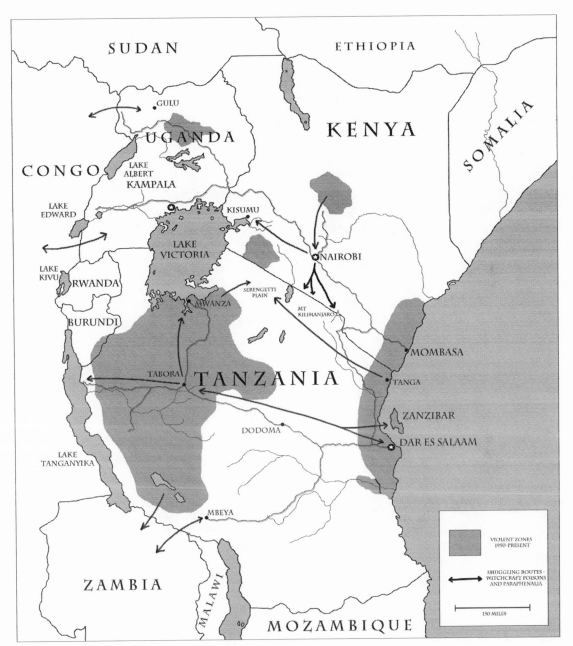

Major smuggling routes for illegal poisons, herbal medicines, amulets and other banned products used to practice witchcraft, as reported by former inspector Gilbert Olonana, Moshi, Tanzania. (Map by Peter C. Allen)

Another form of trade in witchcraft products emerged in the 1980s. In Tanzania I was able to learn something about the trade in human skin from a few students at the University of Dar es Salaam who were studying the violence. Some of the cases came from my old research area in southern Tanzania, around Mbeya.

Following random murders, often of men struggling home alone at night from the beer shops, portions of human skin are taken from the bodies and thereafter prepared and sold to markets in West Africa. In the 1990s and early 2000s the epicenter of the crimes was the area near the borders of Tanzania, Malawi and Zambia, near my home in Rungwe District. The market was driven by the belief that pieces of skin can be used for fertility or strength, protection and good luck.

Investigators pointed to the idea of "sympathetic magic," the belief that the power of the original skin or body part can be transferred from the deceased to the person who acquires it. Part of the psychological power is the "shock effect" that the item carries. Another explanation for the strong market is the belief that human skin serves as a protective charm, like a rabbit's foot in the west. Some Nigerian families are known to pin a swatch of human skin above a baby's crib for security. Police reported the market for a complete skin ranged from $2,400 in East Africa, to $9,600 in Nigeria. The trade moved on trucks over 2000 miles. I remembered what George Kuchar, the salvage diver, had said about the long-distance smuggling of *juju* products in stacks of oil cans.

Beginning in 1999, the Tanzania government took aggressive steps to counter the murders, working first with Zambian and Malawian police and then Interpol, the international investigative agency. Several cases came to court in Mbeya, where a Tanzanian Assistant Police Commissioner, A. Mwayange, testified that "some people superstitiously believe human skin can protect a home from evil spirits and agents of witchcraft. Others believe that when associated with special rituals, human skin can increase harvests and lure more customers into local *pombe* (beer) clubs and shops."

Officials also blamed traditional healers in Mbeya and Rukwa Regions as the organizers who managed the trade after hiring local thugs to do the killing. One outraged Member of Parliament from Mbozi District, Edson Halinga, told the National Assembly that he considered it a fitting punishment for "all 'skinners' proven guilty of the practice to themselves be skinned alive." *

⁙

In spite of the fact that long-distance smuggling is important, the main markets for witchcraft paraphernalia are more local, among thousands of traditional healers across Tanzania, particularly in the market towns and cities. Although I had interviewed a dozen healers and witchfinders like Edom Mwasanguti, I had never studied the products in any detail—the particular herbs, roots, bark, leaves, bones, horns and animal parts. Nor had I learned how these things were used to cure believed witchcraft ailments. Many were trade secrets, and only because of my Tabora friend Solostus Kasubi did a door open on this world.

Kasubi—"everyone calls me Kasubi"—is a gentle, easy-going man in his mid-forties, a physics teacher at the elite Tabora Boys Secondary School who helped me do research in Usagari and other villages when he had time.

"OK," Kasubi said. "I understand you want to see the products used in healing witchcraft-caused ailments. My cousins Saidi and Jaffa Mirisho, they will help."

"Cousins?" I said. "You are not from here. You are from Kahama District. How do you...?"

"Never mind. We agree we are cousins. I get my medicines, he gets my money. Let's go, it's close, near your blacksmith friend at Kipalapala."

Saidi Mirisho's clinic was in an oblong, thatched building decorated inside and out with wall paintings and soon after we arrived at the compound, Mirisho's wife Jaffa joined us, followed by her daughter with a platter of tea and cakes.

"They work together here. There is gender equality," Kasubi whispered. "That's because they are 'modern.' Both of them have some education."

* *Guardian News* (Tanzania), June 18, 1999 and July 7, 1999. In the mid-2000s the skin trade proved to be a precurser to other "sympathetic magic" murders, particularly in Tanzania, Zambia, and parts of the Congo. The murders included an outbreak of albino killings. In these cases albino Africans were killed for skin and body parts, supposedly to create powerful medicines. In Tanzania, an albino woman was appointed to the President's Cabinet to lead a prevention and education campaign.

In the clinic we talked in generalities about their life and their family and when Kasubi thought the time was right, he asked Saidi and Jaffa to make a display of the medicines and artifacts they use in witchcraft cases.

"He says 'OK' for tomorrow…and he agrees to discuss his anti-witchcraft techniques. He learned everything from his grandfather. His father was just a farmer."

The next afternoon, Saidi sat in front of his clinic with a stick and pointed to a dozen items. Kasubi continued to translate, but by now it was clear Saidi spoke some English. Jaffa may have as well. Kasubi picked up another stick and pointed as Saidi talked.

"The red cloth is a standard anti-witchcraft color and is feared by witches. The carved wooden figure is a warrior, a soldier that represents strength—with a shield to protect the patient. The little bamboo fence behind the figure represents a barrier that witches cannot cross. The flywhisk on the left is to dip into liquid medicines and sprinkle on patients. These bottles hold hallucinogenic medicines which Mirisho takes himself to give him a vision of who is bewitching the patient. The rattle on the right warns witches to stay away. The bottles and gourds in the back hold anti-witchcraft medicines."

Artifacts and medicines in the healing compound of Saidi and Jaffa Mirisho used to prevent witchcraft. Tabora, Tanzania, (Author's collection)

Inside, the clinic was divided between a consulting area and a traditional pharmacy with tins and bottles. Most were unmarked but one shelf held only western medicines such as aspirin, smelling salts, lotions, baby powders and tubes of ointment. The clinic walls carried elaborate paintings drawn by both Saidi and Jaffa. Some were similar

Artwork on clinic walls depicts healing myths and legends.

to the 1932 wall paintings from the chief's compound in the Usambara mountains that I had collected years before. After a long discussion, Kasubi cleared his throat.

"Many of these images protect against witchcraft," he said. "The elephants represent strength, as well as social unity, the power in being together. The upside-down figures show that a witch's anti-social behavior can cause illness. The picture of a fence, like the little wooden one outside, is to keep witches and evil spirits away."

"What about the figures holding hands, and the snake?" I asked.

Kasubi and Saidi spoke in Nyamwezi, then Kasubi turned to me.

"He says they are twins, which remind us of bad luck, like a child born feet-first. They are joined at the arms to make them one. The snakes serve as protectors against witchcraft and evil. Mirisho says he is a member of the local bayeye, a snake-handling society. The bird symbolizes the Makai, a spirit possession cult. He says they both give him status and power."

Later, I prodded Kasubi about Saidi's understanding of witchcraft. Kasubi asked the question and again listened for a long time.

"He's good, and very clear about what he believes," Kasubi finally said. "He thinks witchcraft is 'evilness' inside someone, a power that

Saidi Mirisho's pharmacy with western and traditional medicines.

Saidi Mirisho with Jaffa in the position he occupies when treating patients, with anti-witchcraft implements, including the carved statue and medicines seen in his outside display. (Author's collection)

can cause illnesses in others and untimely death or serious misfortune. It is the power that works behind poisoning and behind curses uttered against someone. He believes his manipulation of these charms and beads—and the rhythm of the rattle and drum—actually work to make people relax and feel better. This in turn gives them strength to fight off witchcraft. He and Jaffa do some massage, use oils, sometimes give hallucinogenic drugs to let the patient speak freely. He listens a lot, he does a lot of the same things a psychiatrist does in the west. He also extracts thorns and sews up wounds, but he doesn't cut."

"Cut?" I asked.

"No surgery, no tooth extractions."

"Sick children? Women's health?"

Kasubi posed the question to Jaffa.

"OK," he said. "Jaffa is a traditional midwife and says she received a little training at a Tabora day clinic. She counsels women on their pregnancies and gives them medicines for pain. If they are poor she will go to help with the birth, but most ladies around here go to the local infirmary, which has a birthing bed. She and Saidi both deal with children, but send serious cases to the government hospital. When he had a bike he would take them. Now they walk or wait for a vehicle."

I asked Jaffa about the witchcraft attacks on women in the area, the banishment cases, and some of the violence against women. Didn't she think there was a major gender issue here? When Kasubi translated her answer, the response surprised me.

"Jaffa says these attacks are terrible, but they are against both old men and old women. It's being an elder, not a woman. That is the group that is suffering." *

At that point Kasubi pointed to one of the certificates on the wall and asked Saidi about it.

"It's from a national association of healers. They try to improve healers' work. They set codes of conduct, suggest fees, teach what traditional healers should not do. Saidi says they demand money but don't help him much."

Later that afternoon Kasubi and I sat in a Tabora teahouse and talked over the day. I wanted his views on the gender issue that Jaffa had brought up.

"Isn't it true," I said, "that most witchcraft cases are about conflicts—boundary disputes, land issues, money arguments, honor, and other such fights? So I suspect men and women are equally involved, but in general women in rural Africa have a very hard time. They do most of the field work, get less pay, have less access to education, they can't even insist on condoms when their husbands come home from working elsewhere—possibly with HIV or other VDs. A lot of women are powerless to protect themselves. Maybe that's why they resort to witchcraft practices, like poison, particularly if they are really poor."

"There is something in what you say," Kasubi said. "Sure, your old case—that Mohammadi woman out in Usagari—she was a victim. But overall, I don't agree with you. I'm an African male and I believe in a 'hidden equalizer.'" Kasubi saw I was confused.

"OK," he said. "We Africans find a balance between the sexes. Believe me women here have ways to stay even. Over time families find equilibrium because couples can't live in disequilibrium for long periods. Look at our Nyamwezi women, most of them control the home, control the fields, prepare the food, and give out the food. And think about pastoral women, like the Maasai or the Boran. They may look subservient, but they hold a lot of power. They can ruin their husbands' reputations by giving away free sexual favors and by not keeping it secret. They can really embarrass their husbands. If they don't extend traditional hospitality to his friends—not give tea—it makes the husband a laughing stock for a week."

He paused, and then went on. "I have read about women in Thailand, and those big Brazilian market women who run their businesses, and run their husbands. Think about the 'hidden equalizer.' There is a

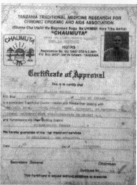

Membership certificates in traditional associations of Tanzania.

balance. That is what is really out here in Africa, even if your western women don't believe it. Sure, it's out here."

The experiences with Saidi and Jaffa Mirisho and the lessons about the paraphernalia they used in modern witchcraft cases continued to intrigue me. A few months later I walked through a big Dar es Salaam market to see what witchcraft products I might actually buy. One, a red powder, smelled like rotten eggs (a threat to be sent through the mail). Another was a gray sauce for women to rub gently on the private parts of an unfaithful husband as he slept (to make him "stick" to his girlfriend). Other items included a monkey paw (for good luck), a black powder for someone's beer pot (to make them sick), tiny carved objects (for good luck) and herbal concoctions to make someone hallucinate and see who is bewitching them—all sold to practice "do it yourself" witchcraft.

During these weeks I also realized that there were a lot of modern art objects and artifacts used for witchcraft purposes. Some were inexpensive carvings, or amulets, flywhisks and bracelets. Makonde art or *shetani* objects were also available, and on the road to the University of Dar es Salaam a colony of Makonde artists worked in open-air shops. In galleries, in Dar, Nairobi and Kampala, there were a lot of things the Makerere art students called *devil art* and *spirit art*.

Aside from the healers' world and the modern art world, the other thing that struck me in the urban areas was how witchcraft was portrayed in the media. Weekly tabloids ran serialized accounts about "How my mother was a witch and a cannibal" or "How a witch stole my virginity." The daily press not only carried stories about witchcraft, particularly when violence was involved, but ran features, editorials and letters to the editor.

Music stalls sold CDs of local disco bands with lyrics about witchcraft. Both Tanzanian and Kenyan TV carried Nigerian films and soap operas about witchcraft. In bookstalls, religious tracts in Swahili, English and some vernacular languages condemned witchcraft as Satan's

"Magic stallion," dark green serpentine carving by Sylvester Mubuyi (48"). (Courtesy of Frank McEwen)

Skeletal Baboon Spirit, light green serpentine carving by Sylvester Mubuyi (11"). (Courtesy of Frank McEwen)

Market art, Mombasa, Kenya. (Author's collection)

Ancestor figure by Sylvester Mubuyi. (Courtesy of Frank McEwen)

Shetani spirit Makonde wood carving, half woman, half animal, (22"). (Author's collection)

Modern Images of Witchcraft   Called 'devil art' or 'spirit art', images that reflect witchcraft beliefs can be found in East African markets and art galleries. In addition to artifacts and amulets, new stone and wood carvings, drawings and paintings exemplify the contemporary art forms.

work and insisted that witches represented an unjust and evil world. Witchcraft was often a part of the daily gossip, the chatter among taxi drivers, between vendors and stall keepers and among the stevedores in the dockside bars. Like sex and soccer, witchcraft was often on the "street radio."

An old friend I looked up on this trip to Dar es Salaam was Bismark Mwansasu, the son of Gordon Mwansasu, the balding chief from Rungwe who shook hands with everyone. Bismark and I had written an article together years before and as we met in a dockside bar I got a lesson on how the idiom of witchcraft can serve as a greeting. The bartender shouted to a dust-covered stevedore as the man came through the door, "*Jambo, mchawi* (Hello, witch)."

The reply was automatic. "*Wewe mchawi* (you're the witch)."

We had other laughs and talked of his doctoral studies in India, his work with the Nyerere Foundation, his teaching at Kivukoni College, and eventually about Chief Gordon. His mood changed.

"My father finished life twelve years ago as a very unhappy man. First,

An example of "spirit art" is a painting entitled "Owl Drums Death" by Peter Mulindwa, Kampala, Uganda (122 cm x 244 cm).

his prize cow was stolen, he believed by a cousin, and the resulting court case split our clan. My cousin's group even tried to renounce our name—the Mwansasu name—and take their mother's name. When my father died suddenly, my siblings wanted to charge the other side with witchcraft. They thought he had been poisoned. I am first-born—I didn't allow it."

When I expressed my admiration for his father, he nodded and changed the subject.

"I remember your interest in the witchcraft business." he said. "I think you knew Edom Mwasanguti the witch-hunter, and the healer Chikanga in Malawi."

"Good memory," I said. "They are long gone, I suppose."

"Yes, dead, but I cannot be generous to either. Mwasanguti died the year before my father, but he had been forced out of witch-finding years before. He was charged with torturing confessions out of people by tying their legs together and twisting the rope with a stick. The local council threatened him with arrest, but it was the young women who finally got him. He was beaten by a gang of fathers."

Bismark saw my confusion. "Some men sent their daughters to work for him, to pay the costs of 'de-witching' their wives or themselves. Edom treated the young women as sex slaves. He had a harem. The fathers got angry, very angry. One tried to burn Edom's house."

"And Chikanga, the healer, in Malawi?" I asked.

"You didn't hear? First, President Banda forced him out of healing and witch-cleansing, as a security risk. Chikanga was gaining a lot of influence and may have had contacts with Banda's political opposition."

"Then what happened?" I asked.

Bismark's gaze now suggested everyone in the world knew the story except me. "He still practised secretly and tried to challenge another healer—a snake handler with a cobra. Chikanga claimed his own powers were greater than those of the healer—and the snake."

"Who won?" I asked, not intending to be flippant.

"The snake. It bit him on the cheek. Chikanga died in two hours."

Later that week, after I had again looked through the Dar es Salaam markets, I gave Bismark a report on the modern evidence of witchcraft I had found—the products, the pamphlets, the music, and in the press.

"Of course," he said. "Uchawi has been urbanized and commercialized. It comes to the city with the healers and there are over 30,000 healers in Dar es Salaam today—if you believe our Health Ministry. That's in a city of over 3 million. Most of these people use witchcraft as a diagnosis because it is profitable—they are selling their own 'protection business.' They want to sell you protection against witchcraft, so they tell you witchcraft is your problem—and that their medicines can help you."

"OK," I said. "But some anthropologists say witchcraft is only a village phenomenon because cities have too great a mixture of ethnic groups. They claim these beliefs wouldn't work across ethnic lines. In the cities the police can stamp it out, the government is too close, even in the market towns."

"They're wrong," he said flatly. "Witchcraft ideas are no longer based only on tribal ideas. Look, there is a new generic form of witchcraft. It's the broad belief that evil powers exist in some humans. It's a tool to settle disputes between migrants, factory workers or office people. An accusation of witchcraft can be general, and it is very powerful. I know, I have worked in this city a long time."

Bismark leaned forward and began to tap the table.

> *"Listen, witchcraft has survived without the need for those wild ideas about flying hags on hyenas."*

"Listen, witchcraft has survived without the need for those wild ideas about flying hags on hyenas. The horror of death, particularly a child's death, believed to be caused by supernatural means...that's the nightmare behind witchcraft. It has been on the street for a long time. It's also a tool for extortion, for intimidation, and these cases happen every day."

"But people hate witchcraft...why, Bismark, why" I said, "does it persist in the face of such opposition? People despise it. The police, the churches—they all stand against it."

Bismark thought for a moment. "You said it earlier. The newspapers, the music, the TV shows with witchcraft soap operas, the 'witch-doctors' racing up and down the sidelines of our soccer games.

Witchcraft ideas are all around. I think a lot of it is due to media hype, the news coverage of witchcraft incidents. The media amplify the damn beliefs. Witchcraft ideas are believed by half-educated people because they are in the press or on the radio. It's a vicious circle—publicity about witchcraft promotes witchcraft."

He raised his glass and waved it in the air. "Let's write another article together, about this modern witchcraft business. Yeah...someone might even read this one."

My final lesson on the economics of witchcraft occurred a few days later in Dar es Salaam when I saw James Rweyemamu, a Tanzanian friend who had recently returned from graduate studies at Syracuse University. We were to meet at the New Africa Hotel and talk to a Nigerian who then worked in Tanzania as a World Bank consultant. I arrived late, but sensed Rweyemamu was already annoyed at Jonathan Ake. Mr. Ake was holding forth on how Tanzania's President Julius Nyerere had wrecked the economy and set the country back at least three decades. A little later they both seemed relieved when I switched the subject to the economic issues surrounding witchcraft beliefs.

"Sure," James said. "Witchcraft is important because it unfortunately keeps everyone in the same stage of development."

"Yes, what you are talking about is 'wealth leveling'," the Nigerian said with finality. "It is one way primitive people use witchcraft to force each other to share, to stay at the same economic level."

"We don't use 'primitive' anymore in East Africa," James said quietly.

Ake managed a weak smile, but kept talking. "In Nigeria the pressure to share wealth, and the fear of witchcraft attack if you don't share it is a big problem. Wage earners often come to their home villages literally with their pockets turned out—to show everyone there is nothing to share. But otherwise, witchcraft at the village-level is meaningless. Village dynamics don't count. Look, it's the big picture—trade, markets, money in the system, industrial growth, agricultural production—that's what's important."

The "village dynamics don't count" comment was like waving a red flag for James Rweyemamu. He had been a part of rural assessment teams in Tanzania that worked on village economic issues and I saw a huge argument coming.

"Let's stay on topic," I pleaded, "the real issue is...."

Rweyemamu didn't hear me. "You're wrong," he said bluntly to Ake. "Village economics is where it all begins and believe me these beliefs are very important. In my village witchcraft threats are used to force people to lend money, to give things away, even to settle boundary disputes. It is an economic weapon and people who claim to have witchcraft powers can make a lot of money."

Ake tried to respond, but Rweyemamu kept talking.

"It starts with the basics. Most of our African villages have poor soils, poor roads, poor rainfall, a lot of poverty, a lot of uncertainty. In my village near Bukoba no one had regular wages, no one had savings, no one paid rent. Cash was often just not around. My family survived on barter, petty trade, small loans, obligations. The two people who worked for my father worked for a few pennies and for a place to sleep and a place at our table."

"OK," Ake said cautiously. "But I want to hear one specific example of how witchcraft hinders progress."

Rweyemamu sensed he had the upper hand. "First, witchcraft is foolishly blamed when things go wrong," he said. "And the real reasons for misfortunes are usually not recognized. I grew up next to a blacksmith who worked a small iron smelter. He blamed witchcraft every time something broke. Whenever there was a crack in a new hoe or he got a cut or a burn, it was witchcraft. Someone was always trying to steal his smelting secrets, he believed—by witchcraft. Same thing with other artisans making clay pots and wooden utensils, or brewing beer. This witchcraft bullshit undermines the economy because it throws up wrong answers to why things go wrong. The mining of gold in central Tanzania, where Miller here has lived, is dangerous because the open-pit trenches can cave in. Instead of building wooden supports, miners think any cave-in is due to witchcraft from other miners and they seek magical protections of all kinds before going into the trenches.

"It is an economic weapon and people who claim to have witchcraft powers can make a lot of money."

"Anyway, all truth is local. It's on the ground. You 'development' types will never understand this because you never do research at the grass roots."

Ake squirmed, but didn't answer. Instead he turned to me.

"And you, sir," Ake said. "Do you have a case where witchcraft hinders progress? A real concrete example?"

"Sure," I said confidently, racking my brain. Then I thought of Mohammadi.

"Sure, I have a case. You can both help me understand a witchcraft case near Tabora—one I have been struggling with for a long time. This very poor woman named Mohammadi was driven out of my village—supposedly for killing a child. Now I am beginning to think she was some kind of economic scapegoat. It was during a time of food shortage, she and her brother held unused land, plus they were outsiders, apparently not very well connected."

Both men nodded and for the first time they seemed to agree on something. Rweyemamu called Mohammadi's situation a "life-boat reality": when shortages occur, people try to get rid of extra mouths to feed, particularly when starvation is possible. The underlying process is village-wide self-preservation, the need to force someone out of the lifeboat to keep it from sinking.

"The economic forces that can drive people to use witchcraft can be very hard to see and not easily understood," Ake said.

"No, I think they can be understood." I said. "A researcher named Ted Miguel has made a three-way connection between witchcraft beliefs, witch killings and certain kinds of economic disaster. It's amazing work, based on a survey of 62 villages in western Tanzania. He found that hundreds of witchcraft killings there were directly tied to droughts or flooding, situations he calls 'economic shocks.' He developed an excellent profile of the victims. They were usually women, an average age of fifty-seven, their average education four years. The victims were very poor in terms of land, savings, livestock and material goods. Two-thirds professed the traditional Sukuma-Nyamwezi religion, not Christianity or Islam. And—this is amazing—in a majority of the cases a family member or near neighbor was involved in the killings."

"The underlying process is village-wide self-preservation, the need to force someone out of the lifeboat to keep it from sinking.

"Where did you find this guy? What else did he say?" Rweyemamu said.

"He's an American researcher," I said. "He worked in both Tanzania and Kenya. He also found that very few villagers made the connection between the witchcraft murders and the reasons for the murders, that is, the economic realities. They did blame 'witches' for causing individual sickness and death and for killing cattle, but not for the drought or flood that, in fact, statistically triggered the murders. Drought or flooding was directly correlated with the dates of the murders. When these natural problems became severe, witch killings increased. Other kinds of murders, such as crimes of passion, murder for theft, were not tied to the economic shocks.

"Even with this 'economic shock' explanation," I continued, "what I personally do not understand is how villagers—in large numbers, across a vast area—can justify the killing of old ladies. This is enormous inhumanity. These are grandmothers who in better times were loved and revered."

"It is a 'lifeboat' reality again...no room in the boat." Rweyemamu said. "Under dire economic circumstances some people believe it necessary to eliminate an individual—murder for group survival. Who must die? How the community justifies the killing—those are the basic questions. Naming someone a witch solves both."

"OK, let me get this straight." I said. "Bad weather equals drought or flooding. These are serious economic shocks that cause a village-wide fear of disaster. The fear causes a reaction. That reaction leads to an agreement to eliminate someone because there are not enough resources—food, water, land, whatever. Killing old ladies is difficult unless they can be seen as evil. Witches are evil. Old ladies are scapegoats. Witchcraft is the justification."

I thought my summary would prompt further debate, but it didn't. We sat in silence. Almost out of embarrassment I decided to bring up something I had been mulling over for a long time.

"OK," I said. "Here's a question. Is there any good that comes from witchcraft? A lot of villagers excuse witchcraft, even violence tied to witchcraft, if it rids the village of a tyrannical leader. Isn't that a 'greater good,' a clearing out of bad people? What if witchcraft accusations eliminate unproductive people or force them out of the village? In fact the village will use fewer resources—like your 'lifeboat' theory—and that helps the greater good."

Ake sat in silence, shaking his head as if he did not know what to say about the question. Rweyemamu paused for just a moment, then dismissed me.

"Don't even open that box, my friend. The harm of witchcraft is far greater than any good it might do."

8

Political Witchcraft

1999–2000

Rodger Yeager, American field researcher in Tanzania
John Mboniko, Police Commander, Tabora, Tanzania
Magdalena Kasubi, grandmother, Kahama District
Alice Lakwena, Lord's Resistance Army, Uganda
John Kony, Lord's Resistance Army, Uganda
Charles Macharia, librarian, *The Nation*, Nairobi, Kenya

The idea that witchcraft beliefs serve as a "hidden government" was the topic on the table. I was arguing that witchcraft practices are like Mafia activities. They are illegal and often violent and profit-oriented, a *soto-governo* or gang-like under-government that thumbs its nose at civil authority. Witchcraft provides an alternative system of justice. I had argued all this with, I thought, considerable eloquence.

My friend Rodger Yeager shook his head, and waved his chopsticks. "Monkey piss, just plain monkey piss! Get off the abstract grand theory, Miller, and just report the damn cases. Anyway, look, the problem is not the hidden politics, it is understanding what these governments can do about witchcraft. That's the big problem. What should their policy be? And let's get out of here...pay the damn bill for a change."

The sleepy waiter in the old Chinese restaurant near the Dar es Salaam train station looked relieved. He had been trying to follow our conversation, perhaps as a spy for Beijing, but had given up and gone to sleep in the corner.

Earlier, Yeager, a political scientist who had done village-level research in western Tanzania, did agree that witchcraft cases could be very political. My banishment case of Mohammadi was an example of how a vigilante group can usurp government power and hold an illegal trial. The poisoning case of old Chief Mdeka was a political assassination, explained by the villagers to themselves as witchcraft. A municipal employee I knew in Kenya was jailed for the practice of witchcraft against other employees and for keeping potions in his desk. Near my village in Rungwe, a tax collector I knew was brought to court for intimidating people who refused to pay school fees and local taxes. He had threatened to tattoo recalcitrant villagers, and publicly displayed amulets to protect himself from their counter-witchcraft. In all East African countries, including Malawi and Zambia, political parties employed witchcraft to gain power and undermine local opponents, often by using their Youth Wings as enforcers.

Yeager and I agreed that witchcraft at the national level is a drama on a much larger stage. In recent years, since 2000, all East African Parliaments have debated changes to make the anti-witchcraft laws more effective, and earlier, all governments have appointed national commissions to investigate witchcraft problems, particularly extensive witch-hunting and episodes of witch-killing. Most national leaders have held rallies and preached the "stop witchcraft" messages. One large public harangue by President Daniel Moi of Kenya blamed British colonialism for promoting witchcraft as their way to control and suppress Africans.

My talks with Rodger Yeager helped me see that there are at least three ways witchcraft influences national politics in East Africa. The most common is when a small witchcraft incident blows up into a national event. A second is the state using witchcraft for its own ends, as in Idi Amin's state-sponsored terrorism. A third is when a rebel group uses witchcraft against an established state.

First, an example of a major incident that started small occurred in Kenya surrounding the witch-hunting work of Kajiwe (Little Stone) on the Kenya coast. The same pattern was seen in Kenya's Kisii District following a series of local witchcraft-inspired murders and in Lango District, Uganda, after a local witch-hunting episode. The best known example, however, of an isolated incident mushrooming into a national event occurred in western Tanzania. The national press called it "Tanzania's Silent Holocaust."

For me, the "Holocaust" story started in the 1970s, soon after my friend Commander Ben Mpazi was dismissed for failing to suppress witch killings in Tabora. The next police operation covered the whole western region. It was called "Operation Mauaji (against killing)," and was launched with the mandate to stop witchcraft murders at all costs. It collapsed when heavy-handed police interrogations led to the deaths of twenty suspects while in police custody. As a direct result, two cabinet members and a regional police commissioner resigned and several police officers were tried, convicted and jailed. Operation Mauaji was abandoned.

In the mid-1980s another investigative commission was started, this time by Tanzania's ruling political party, the Chama Cha Mapinduzi (CCM). Its 1988 report was so shocking that the problem earned the name "Tanzania's Silent Holocaust." The commission found that between 1970 and 1984 some 3,693 people were murdered for "practicing witchcraft" (1,407 men, 1,286 women). Nearly two-thirds of the

The national press called it "Tanzania's Silent Holocaust."

cases were from the Mwanza-Shinyanga-Tabora region, the area in which I had lived in the 1960s and for a short time in the 1970s. Again, in the late 1990s, the Ministry of Home Affairs shocked the nation with information that over 3,000 more people in the region were killed as witches between 1994 and 1998. Many of the victims were women who suffered from red eyes caused by smoke from cooking fires—red eyes were believed to be a sign of witchcraft powers.*

Just after these events, on a trip to Tabora, I was able to talk to the new District Police Commander in Tabora, the man in the job Ben Mpazi had held years before. Whether it was because I knew Mpazi or because he saw me as a friend concerned about one of Tanzania's big problems, John Mboniko was remarkably candid. We met in his office in the old German fort that overlooked Tabora town and the rolling countryside. He was a big, broad-shouldered man in a starched white uniform and he sat remarkably straight at his desk.

"What you called the 'Holocaust' business is a very complicated story," Mboniko said. "A lot of these murders are carried out by village militias or home guards, called 'sungusungu,' formed in the 1970s by the government itself to curtail night prowling and cattle theft. Many sungusungu have become far too powerful. They make their own rules, and give out fines for things like drunkenness or adultery. Some conduct illegal trials, decide who is a witch and either banish them or arrange for their murder."

---

*Witchcraft-related murders in Western Tanzania were documented both in the Tanzanian press and by a non-governmental women's media group. For example between 1970-1984, some 1407 men were killed as witches versus 1286 women in the Mwanza and Shinyanga region of Western Tanzania. By 1998 *The Guardian* of Tanzania again pinpointed this region as a center of witchcraft violence and blamed the cases on land dispute, (boundary and ownership issues), property inheritance, and "concubinage" meaning conflicts between co-wives in large families. (*The Guardian*, December 21, 1998). The male-female ratio of those accused of witchcraft in the author's study of witchcraft cases reported in the East African press between 1960-2010 was similar to the 1970-1984 data, although the ratios were reversed, in that 52% of those accused were women, 48% men.

"A kind of shadow government?" I asked.

"Sure...but just in their villages. They don't link up. They don't try to attack the central government."

"Let me be sure I understand," I said. "The government established these *sungusungu* groups for village protection, and started thousands across the country, as a home-protection campaign. Gradually some of these became vigilante groups who run the villages, even condemn people to death."

"That's right," Mboniko said. "It's a political plague, very hard to stop."

Remarkably, he then began to list some of the same issues that Judge Kawawa had given me years before. "This is a vast region," he said. "There are hundreds and hundreds of remote villages, no police coverage, no vehicles, no petrol, no local cooperation. A lot of the killings are not reported unless someone walks miles to a police post."

Commander Mboniko had four staff officers waiting outside his door for a meeting so we agreed to meet the next day. As I stood to leave, he rummaged on his desk, then picked up three metal arrowheads, each about three inches long, shiny and barbed. He held them out in the palm of his hand.

"My current problem," he said. "The local *sungusungu* groups around here *demand* that all homesteads have bows and arrows for protection to shoot witches or thieves. Then they force people to buy poison for the tips of these damn things. Anyway, we meet tomorrow."

That afternoon, just on a whim, I decided to visit a blacksmith I knew near the Kipalapala mission, near the healers Saidi and Jaffa Mirisho. Sure enough, Issa Ndima was busy pounding out arrowheads, knives and small spears, as well as cow bells, all for the *sungusungu*. We talked about the processes and he gave me three arrowheads as a gift. He said the *sungusungu* was a very good idea. It gave him a lot of work.

Aside from Commander Mboniko and blacksmith Ndima, my only other experience with *sungusungu* was through my friend Kasubi, the physics teacher who had helped me do field research in Tabora. One morning, Kasubi failed to show up as planned and it was not until that evening that he could explain the problem. His mother, a widow named Magdalena, living to the north in Kahama District, had been

Equipment to protect the homestead: spear heads, knives, cowbells, and small spear. Local militia in western Tanzania encouraged all homestead owners to have bows and arrows as defense against thieves, witches and night prowlers.

Blacksmith Issa Ndima, Kipalapala, near Tabora, Tanzania, 2005. (Author's collection)

accused of witchcraft. Her grandchildren had overheard a men's *sungusungu* group call her a witch and discuss ways to dispatch her. Terrified, Magdalena contacted Kasubi's sister who then alerted Kasubi.

At five, before dawn that morning he had boarded the northbound bus for Kahama town, found a rural taxi in the market and gone straight to his home village. Even before seeing his mother, Kasubi sat down with the *sungusungu* leaders.

"I told them they were good men, a diligent home guard, all trying to protect the village from night prowlers and witches. But then I argued that they too, the 'home guard' themselves, would someday be old and someday be candidates for elimination just like other elders in the village."

"A brave approach," I said. " How did they react?"

"They were OK. I think they were so amused at the reference to themselves as future witches that they agreed to protect her, for a while. I left packets of tea and two hundred shillings ($16) and promised to come back. I left a 'bribe.' But my mother is definitely in the wrong group—she is old and poor and widowed, and is seen by her neighbors as a drain on the village resources. Very little comes from her garden and she is always asking people to bring her firewood or carry her water pails. She is very demanding. I know! I'm her son."

"Is she safe?" I asked. Kasubi paused and his face clouded over.

"For the moment, but I spoke to my sister about moving her to one of the government camps along the Tabora-Mwanza rail line. The ones where accused witches are guarded by police. They are terrible, terrible places but she will be safe."

"I don't understand these type of murders," I said. "Do the same men who make the judgments do the killings?"

"Not usually," Kasubi replied. "The murders are assigned to small gangs. Some of them are just local thugs, but some are secret societies, terror cells that can be activated for money. Sometimes they are the same people who are in the *sungusungu*, the home guards. Sometimes not. Only the insiders know."

At that point Kasubi gave me a troubled look. "You know, as a scientist and teacher, I don't believe in this witchcraft business. It's rubbish and I tell my students that too. But most of my neighbors believe it. Norman, if I want to live here, I have to keep that in mind."

A second major pattern in the political uses of witchcraft is when a government itself employs occult ideas for its own purposes. One example was Idi Amin's state-run terrorism. Another occurred in Kenya under the rubric of the "Devil Cults." This was a bizarre set of claims by the government of Daniel Moi that satanic forces were loose in the country, preying on children and leading to ritual cannibalism and other horrendous acts. The situation finally came to a head after nearly five years when a document was released entitled "The Presidential Commission of Inquiry into Devil Worship." It described ritual murders, witchcraft ceremonies and other "satanic" practices, including human sacrifice and cannibalism, supposedly done using witchcraft powers. Although no evidence was released, supposedly the victims were children who had been ritually killed for their body parts in order to restore health to the perpetrators.

Shocking to all Kenyans was the fact the President's report accused several international religious groups of satanic practices. All had worked in Kenya for years. The groups included the Jehovah's Witnesses, Hare Krishnas, Latter Day Saints (Mormons), Freemasons, Christian Scientists and the Theosophical Society. The report suggested all were involved in human sacrifice, snake handling, blood drinking, sex orgies, cannibalism and other rituals.

Several prominent African Christian clergymen joined the public debate and suggested the devil cults *proved* there was a resurgence of witchcraft in Kenya. That the government continued the investigation for nearly five years, and released the report only under public pressure, suggests it was a political hoax. Many observers believed that Daniel Moi allowed supporters to orchestrate a rumor campaign about devil cults to take public focus off his own political problems. When these events took place in the mid-1990s he had grown increasingly unpopular, due mainly to police repression, favoritism, and alleged elite corruption in the face of growing poverty among the masses. (Moi was reported to be one of the ten richest men in the world with most of his wealth in Switzerland.) Specifically he faced a major strike in the civil service.

Whatever the deeper truth, the stories did create widespread alarm and fear, and in fact diverted enough attention from Kenya's economic realities to allow Daniel Moi to survive. For some, however, the costs were high, including two old women in Gachami, central Kenya, who were doused with petrol by hysterical villagers and burned to death as witches. They had been accused of trying to kidnap children for satanic rituals.

Daniel arap Moi,
President of Kenya,
1978-2002.

PRESIDENTIAL "BIOGRAPHY"

Earlier on the basis of a book I had written, called *Kenya: The Quest for Prosperity*, I was invited by Daniel Moi's Foreign Minister, Elijah Mwangale, to meet the President and discuss writing his biography. At that point Moi had been in power some six years and charges against him of brutality and corruption were yet to surface. I was flattered and immediately began to research the remarkable trajectory of his life from a herdsboy, initially schooled at an American mission station in central Kenya to local counselor, National Legislative Counselor, Vice-President under Jomo Kenyatta, and then, in 1978, President of Kenya.

At the State House, when I was ushered in to meet him, Moi was sitting on a long couch behind a coffee table. Elijah Mwangale was nearby in an easy chair. They both stood. I was greeted by the President with a faint smile and brusque handshake, and waved to an easy chair next to him. Moi came right to the point.

"My Minister here has shown me your book on Kenya. Would you do another, a biography of my Presidency?" He paused and looked at Mwangale without expression. "What would you want—what are your conditions to do this?"

I had anticipated the question. It would take three months of research, four taped private interviews, a chance to visit in his home and meet his wife, to be with him at public events, to see him on at least one trip to a village. I needed to understand him in both formal and informal settings. I wanted to hear what he thought about Kenya's international relations, about Kenya's economic progress, what he thought about the role of the church, particularly about the problems of witchcraft. This would be a serious, in-depth biography, starting in his early years, all about his political rise through the Legislative Council, his VP years, then through his Presidency. If it were well done, I thought Oxford University Press might be interested.

"No, my Presidency only," Moi said abruptly. "I want these years only. My Presidency, that's all."

At that point he made an expansive gesture with his right hand and knocked the red rose out of his left lapel. It flew up in the air and onto the carpet. All three of us scrambled to the floor, all three on one knee. I reached the rose first, picked it up and put it on the coffee table. Mwangale helped the President back to his seat.

"No," the President said, reaching for his handkerchief and wiping his brow. "Two meetings. Two months. Mwangale will give you the material. I want a lot of pictures."

There was a tap on the wood-paneled door behind Mwangale and a Colonel in a full dress uniform stepped in, bowed and said that the President's motorcade was ready to take him to Nyeri.

"Mwangale will get back to you," the President said as he stiffly shook my hand.

Minister Mwangale did call the next morning. The President didn't want witchcraft questions. He didn't like the idea that witchcraft was a problem in Kenya. They were talking over my other suggestions. He would get back to me.

He never did. I learned later the witchcraft question had derailed the project, at least my part in it. Two months later a ghost-written Presidential biography appeared in Nairobi as a public relations puff about Moi, a dreary, badly written aggrandizement (with pictures) that was pushed by government agents into all the bookstores and market stalls.

Another example of government-sanctioned witchcraft activity occurs from time to time in national elections. The election-rigging case I had seen first-hand on the Rungwe district tea estate had parallels at the national level. In one, a contested election I followed, the former Vice President of Kenya, Oginga Odinga, was charged in court "to have committed acts of superstition and witchcraft to influence people to vote for Mr. J. Hezekiah Origo in Bondo constituance." The case was widely believed to be a part of the government's campaign to discredit Odinga.

Another high-level case involved oathing and election-rigging. Here, Dr. Musikari Kombo from Webuye, western Kenya, was charged with administering a traditional oath, the *Khalia Shilulu* to insure he got votes. The ritual involved drinking a mixture of herbs, sheep's blood, and Kombo's bath water and thereafter uttering commitments to vote for Kombo or die. He was found guilty and his election nullified. Although he was barred from ever standing for election, the national party later pushed through a constitutional amendment that allowed him to run again. Before he had been convicted, Dr. Kombo told the judge that he "did not believe in witchcraft, sorcery or charms and as a person who had undergone modern education, he found the allegation of oathing to be repulsive, repugnant and against his personal and moral norms." *

A third major way witchcraft beliefs are used politically at the national level is via rebel activity against established governments. Examples in recent years include groups in Liberia, Sierra Leone, Ivory Coast, Congo, Angola, Somalia and northern Uganda. The rebels are often renegades who make a better living in the bush than they could as poor farmers. Most live off the land, maraud for food, smuggle diamonds or some commodity for weapons, raid convoys, and intimidate remote villages. Some of the glue that binds the groups is *juju* or *maribou* in West Africa, and similarly, witchcraft or spirit vengeance in East and Central Africa.

My firsthand experience along this line occurred while driving with three others to a UN-sponsored wildlife workshop in Mbarara, Uganda. We were stopped by a Ugandan army sergeant with

* East African Standard, 5/29/2000

a dozen very young recruits and told to wait for a military escort. There had been a raid by the Lord's Resistance Army on a nearby village and eleven children had been kidnapped to serve either as LRA soldiers or sex slaves for the officers. The Uganda army recruits at our roadblock, however, were unconcerned about any danger. Some pointed their guns playfully at each other, while others aimed at birds in the trees.

"Child soldiers on both sides," my friend said as we watched a boy in a baggy uniform lean his rifle against a tree to urinate. "Look, he is not much taller than the rifle."

Because of my interest in witchcraft, I had followed the Lord's Resistance Army story for a long time. Supposedly to rid Uganda of witches and widespread evil, a rebellion against the Ugandan Government began in 1987. It was led by a 27-year-old self-proclaimed prophet, an ex-prostitute who called herself Alice Lakwena ("messenger from God" in the local vernacular). She initially led 600 disaffected farmers and ex-soldiers in an uprising that reached within forty miles of the nation's capital. Over time, Lakwena persuaded other rebel groups to follow her, claiming her magic and anti-witchcraft powers would bring success.

Lord's Resistance Army leader, Alice Lakwena. (Reuters)

She gave her soldiers "magic" potions to rub on their skins to make them impervious to bullets, and ordered them to fight standing straight up. At one of the major battles against trained government troops, at Corner Kilak, her soldiers showed fanatical bravery—but lost badly. Among the dead were dozens of tiny wire helicopters and tanks that the prophet had said would magically grow larger and help in the attacks.

Rebel beliefs were a mixture of local rituals and ideas from Roman Catholicism, a legacy of the Verona Fathers missionary group that had been in the Acholi region of Uganda for over seventy years. Initially the use of magic seemed to be confined to the prophet's Holy Spirit Battalion, but several other rebel assaults were led by men singing Christian hymns and waving Bibles. Alice Lakwena was wounded in one of the skirmishes and fled to Kenya, only to be arrested near the border and jailed for a long period in a Kenyan prison, probably as a favor to the Ugandan authorities.

In hindsight, Lakwena used two basic occult ploys. She convinced her followers that she had divine status and could cleanse people of witchcraft. She also used a "transformation" myth that I had seen before, in this case claiming she could turn wire toys into real weapons. Most of her recruits were desperately poor, uneducated young men.

After Lakwena's capture, John Kony, a relative, took over the LRA and built it into a major rebel force. Marauding across parts of northern Uganda, raiding into the Congo and taking support from the Sudanese to be a buffer against Uganda's government, Kony's LRA has existed for over twenty years as lawless brigands, constantly out-maneuvering Uganda's attempts to subdue him.*

Another political rebellion that used witchcraft ideas began in Kenya in the late 1990s in the guise of an anti-government vigilante group known as Mungiki. The term "Mungiki" was probably derived from Mungai, the Kikuyu god believed to reside on Mt. Kenya. Among things Mungiki hoped to revive in their neo-traditional movement was the belief in witchcraft. Their activities echoed the Mau Mau land rebellion of the 1950s in that both organizations advocated the overthrow of Kenya's government.

My first encounter with Mungiki happened one warm evening outside the old *Daily Nation* newspaper offices in downtown Nairobi. Across the street, in the ranks of mud-splattered taxis waiting for fares into the rural areas, a fight broke out among drivers. Fists were flying, some men were climbing over the cars, others were standing on the hoods with sticks. I watched two teenage boys smash the windshield of a black Peugeot taxi with cricket bats.

"What's happening?" I asked the old news vendor near the front door.

"They are fighting, Bwana, fighting over the taxi routes. The Mungiki boys are fighting to help some of the drivers. They want to force others to pay them for protection...or pay for rights to drive to Kiambu and Thika."

"What's Mungiki?" I asked.

* When Alice Lakwena died in Kenya in 2007, the LRA, then under John Kony had fought the longest guerrilla war in Africa's modern history.

"A gang. They demand oaths, they don't like anyone to be disloyal. They have beheaded three."

I started to ask more, but he waved me away.

"If they see me talking to a European, they might hurt me. Go up and see your friend Charles the librarian. He will tell you."

As I jogged up the stairs, it struck me the old man knew more about me than I knew about him.

"The old man is OK," Charles said. "He thinks he is the eyes and ears of the press. Some of the reporters pay him for information, for tips, that's all. He knows most Europeans come to the library for the clipping files."

I breathed easier. I had known Charles Macharia since he was a political science student at the University of Nairobi, and now, at the end of his work day, he was happy to talk.

"Oh, Mungiki," he said. "Its purpose is to liberate Kenya. They are upset about the corruption and wealth of our political elite and they want to unite the masses against the government. Today they are Kikuyu from central Kenya but they hope to recruit others. They are anti-Christian and anti-western and want to restore traditional African values, including stronger beliefs in witchcraft. They push a return to female circumcision, traditional food, traditional Kikuyu religion.

"But these guys are rough," he continued. "They have executed at least a dozen people who refused to take their initiation oaths or who tried to quit Mungiki. They raid villages to burn the houses of those who oppose them, hold street demonstrations, even attack women for modern hairstyles or for wearing short skirts. From our photo files, most Mungiki are unemployed young men with dreadlocks. They also recruit among the thousands of teenagers and homeless kids in Nairobi."

Charles got us tea, then showed me to a table to read the files. "Start here," he said. "Remember Mungiki is just one vigilante group. I will show you some others."

In a few minutes he was back. One file was marked "Mwakenya," another "Vaya," yet another, "Hyena Cults." Then files came on the "Baghdad Boys" and the "Teheran Boys." The first three were secret societies that I had known and talked to Judge Kawawa about years ago, but the last two were new to me.

"They all play with witchcraft ideas"

"They all play with witchcraft ideas," Charles said, "mostly to intimidate people or to extort money for their political agenda. Most claim witch-hunting is one of their special powers, like the 'born-again' churches."

"Members of Parliament?" I exclaimed, reading an article in one of the files. "Are these private militias headed by people in Parliament?"

"Nobody can prove that," Charles said. "But some bigwigs in Parliament definitely have gangs and the bigger factions have followers who could be called a private militia. They are all organized along tribal lines...sorry, ethnic lines."

Charles said there had been a "ceasefire" with the government when a key Mungiki leader converted to Christianity and opened his own "born-again" church. But the peace was short-lived and atrocities soon escalated, as did government raids on known sect members in Nairobi's shantytowns. Human rights organizations criticized both Mungiki for the wanton killings and the Kenya security forces for excessive brutality against innocent citizens.

"But you know," Charles said, "Africa has hundreds of vigilante groups headed by warlords who claim to have seen God, spoken to God, or been in direct touch with Jesus. Mungiki is not the only group that pushes that shit."

"How do these groups get started?" I asked. "I don't understand their origin."

"Across Africa? Most rise from political upheavals, rebellions, coups or the aftermath of a local war. Like your Lord's Resistance Army in Uganda. Others fill a power vacuum caused when a one-party systems fails, a situation that has happened a lot in Africa. But at the core? They succeed because they rely on traditional interpretations of how the world works. They use the idea that there are evil spirits. Once that idea is in place—that spirits of evil exist—it becomes a way of thinking, an ideology. It is a closed, self-encased system that provides all the answers. If you say witchcraft does not exist, you may be a witch."

"That explains a lot," I said. "And I am beginning to see why African governments are so concerned about witchcraft in politics."

"Of course! And you know why? Because witchcraft strikes at the heart of governments' ability to govern. A government's key function is to first provide security. Right? Witchcraft beliefs promote fear and insecurity. National leaders in the capital know they can't control what happens in the village. Why? Because witchcraft is a weapon of control for the people who run the village, the 'big men'—sometimes 'big women'—use the threat of witchcraft to intimidate the hell out of people, to maintain power. That's the answer. Witchcraft is a serious threat to stable government, all across Africa."

I thought of my friend Rodger Yeager, waving his chopsticks in the air and asking what the governments can do about witchcraft, what their policy solutions might be. I asked Charles Macharia.

"You mean if our leaders had the political will to attack the problem, what would they propose? Maybe first look to South Africa or Ghana, who have done some practical stuff. Train local police specifically to understand witchcraft cases. South Africa has special units to investigate these things. And make village leaders know they will be prosecuted if witchcraft violence pops up in their villages. Work to establish a tiny welfare system for the elderly so that the old ladies are worth something, have a little income, a kind of 'insurance money' for elders. Also, really try to develop a curriculum for the primary schools to stop witchcraft. Hell, if Uganda can start an HIV/AIDS education program in their primary schools why can't we start anti-witchcraft education? We need to break these myths that there is some evil spirit power out there."

I wanted to press him on how he thought African kids learn witchcraft ideas, but Charles was impatient to go. He put away the teacups, locked the library and we walked down the stairs together. Outside, he took a paper and gave a tip to the old vendor (who nodded to me as if he knew everything we had said upstairs).

"Go see Patrick Ndeka at Nairobi Hospital," he said. "Dr. Ndeka is a very nice man."

9

Lessons Learned

2003–2004

Patrick Ndeka, psychiatrist, Nairobi, Kenya
Ali Bakari, ten-year-old boy, Usagari, Tanzania
Welelo Mkombe, ex-convict, Usagari, Tanzania

I found Dr. Patrick Ndeka at the Nairobi hospital with his feet on his desk, reading a journal, glasses perched on the end of his nose. He smiled, jumped up, shook hands, sat down and put his feet back on his desk. Although we had an appointment, I knew only that he was a Kenya-born psychiatrist trained in the UK who treated witchcraft cases and lectured occasionally on the topic at the University of Nairobi. On the phone he had shown an immediate interest in talking about witchcraft.

Early in the conversation I brought up the idea of "hidden powers" and the possible parallels between African witchcraft ideas and western ideas of the paranormal, things like clairvoyance, extrasensory perception, and precognition. Ndeka studied me, then began polishing his glasses.

"Sorry," he said. "The paranormal is nonsense. Virtually nothing has been proven. It's all intuition. Some people can master details, make predictions, figure the probabilities. It's called wisdom. Nothing supernatural going on. In fact, there is no 'supernatural.' Everything in the world is natural."

"But...but," I said. "Millions of people believe in hidden powers. Ideas of spirits, ghosts, voodoo-like powers. Can millions be wrong? Don't some of your patients claim such powers?"

"Claim...yes, of course, and many also believe they are bewitched by someone with those powers. I have never found evidence of such things. Never!" There was no hesitation. Ndeka flatly rejected the paranormal, everything supernatural.

"Divination," I protested, "the business of foretelling has been in African societies for eons—the ability to predict, to know the future, the idea of precognition."

"Doesn't exist," he repeated. "It is experience, insight, intuition and a lot of trickery and fakery. Paranormal ideas can be, or will be, explained by science. I believe in science, not ghost stories."

I thought of the hardest question I could.

"OK. Then how does witchcraft really work? What's the process, what's the lesson?"

He didn't blink. "First you need to come up with analogies, with parallels. Witchcraft is like a community-level morality play with actors. In the end it is a process of social manipulation, a mechanism. It is not a religion with a central dogma. It is more like a local form of voodoo, a system of thought, a local-level fear system."

I held my head in mock frustration.

"OK...I'll be more concrete," Ndeka said, reaching for a big yellow pad. "Look, witchcraft is a *reaction*. It is the *by-product* of a tragic event. The secondary effect of some misfortune, like a ripple from a pebble thrown into a pond. It's a reaction that triggers other things, other activities."

"...witchcraft is a fear system."

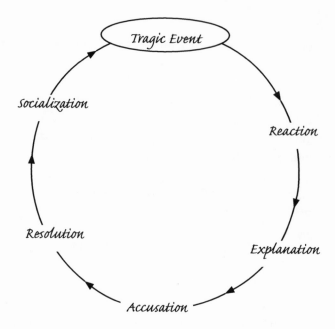

Dr. Patrick Ndeka's sketch of the "witchcraft process" which he saw as a by-product of a tragic event.

He began to draw a little circle. "Like this. It is a cycle. A vicious cycle. A 'cycle-circle.'" He smiled, pleased with his word play, then scribbled words on his pad and handed it to me.

"That explains witchcraft, that's what witchcraft is," Ndeka said with even more confidence. "It's a process *and* a practice. It starts with a tragic event, which leads to the suspicion of witchcraft, then to a search for someone to blame."

"And then?" I asked.

"An *accusation*! An accusation is the heart of the matter. That's when the gauntlet is thrown down in this whole business. Then, some kind of action follows. Somebody is attacked, wounded, beaten or banished, maybe even killed. The accusation is the heart of the whole business."

He paused, then continued. "Or maybe there is a delay. The individuals run away or the case smolders and a feud begins between two families, to be settled some other day. The final phase is passing the beliefs on, teaching the next generation. It's called socialization, teaching the young."

At that moment a nurse appeared at the door. She looked stern. There was a patient waiting and two staff meetings after that. Ndeka jumped up, grabbed some papers, dropped them, shook my hand, picked up the papers and rushed to the door.

"Call me when you come back from the bush. Let's work on this again!"

Walking to the parking lot I realized that Ndeka's "process" idea, his circle of events, was a good general explanation of how modern witchcraft cases work. What I still did not understand was the last phase, how Africans pass witchcraft ideas to the next generation. A week later, 450 miles south of Nairobi, a partial answer came from a ten-year-old boy.

In Usagari, my "home" village in western Tanzania, Ali, the grandson of my friend Saidi Bakari, sat eyeing the cakes in the local teahouse. I was talking to his father, Mbela, about how witchcraft ideas are kept alive. Mbela pointed to his son.

"Through him. Ali knows *uchawi*. Sure, he knows. Ask him."

For an orange Fanta, we got Ali to sit still and Mbela told him to tell me what witches are like. Ali carefully put down his drink, and started counting on his fingers. Mbela translated.

"They eat people, they can fly upside down, they can be *fisi* (hyenas)." He paused then reached for his Fanta. "They have red eyes, they can hurt you, and make you sick."

"Ali, how do you know this?" I asked.

He shrugged, still eyeing the cakes. I got him one and paid the half-shilling but before Ali could answer his father spoke: "His grandmother teaches him. He hears us talking about incidents. He saw a ceremony about witchcraft, the cleansing of our neighbor. He has seen clay dolls and little carvings of witches the elders use to tell stories."

"When did he learn these ideas?" I asked.

"Very early, when he started to walk," Mbela said.

"*Witches eat people, fly upside down, they can be hyenas.*"

Ali Bakari, age 10, Usagari, Tanzania. (Author's collection)

Over that summer I got to know Ali Bakari. He was a winsome lad who could count to ten, write his name, speak some Swahili and read a few words in English. The village teacher, however, said he was a poor student, often tired in class, particularly in dry seasons when food was scarce. She said he was not likely to learn much science, which meant he was unlikely to learn anything that challenged his witchcraft ideas.

I did, however, realize Ali was teaching me something important. Like millions of African children, he had learned about witchcraft as a toddler watching family activities, listening to stories and hearing parents discuss a witchcraft incident. This was classic "informal learning," the ideas taken in with the sights and sounds and smells of his homestead, pressed into his mind with vivid feelings. Witchcraft was in fact built in him as a basic emotion, a basic reaction.

Even if Ali had gotten an education that would counter the witchcraft ideas, even if he began to question witchcraft, this would not happen until he had been exposed to a system that used evidence and looked for proof, a system of thinking based on science. This could not begin in the best of circumstances until middle school, long after he had been steeped in witchcraft thinking. Witchcraft ideas were based on deep emotion. For millions upon millions of kids like Ali, emotion trumps reason.

While in Usagari village with little Ali, I again met Welelo Mkombe, the woman who had spent time in prison for attempting to poison old Chief Mdeka. We had met several times in the past, but this time I made a point to buy charcoal from her son and eggs from her in the market. When my friend Kasubi came out from Tabora on the weekend to help with the field research I asked him to ask her if she would talk to us.

"I want to know about the night the chief died," I said. "It is the 'death by suggestion' idea we have talked about. After she put the powder in the chief's beer pot, did she tell him—actually tell him—there was poison there?"

"That's all?" Kasubi asked. "Nothing more?"

"That's the main question. But other details would be good. How

"There is still a mystery about his death. What killed him?"

old was she, how did the chief treat her? Did she believe, as the villagers did, that she had witchcraft powers? But I'm mainly trying to solve the puzzle of how he died. There is still a mystery about his death. What killed him?"

Later that day we gathered in the shade at Welelo's hut, near her tethered goat and a flock of brown chickens. She and her sister had agreed to meet us and, when we arrived, the sister shook hands and curtseyed, and then disappeared into their hut to stoke a fire and make tea. Kasubi began by saying we were her friends and simply wanted to understand the old case. We both suspected she had been badly treated. Welelo listened, watching us with suspicion. Then something Kasubi said opened the floodgates. Yes, she welcomed the chance to talk and to set the record straight. After a long dialogue, Kasubi translated in a low voice.

"She was eighteen…the fourth wife. Yes, the chief was sexually demanding, but he did not hurt her or beat her. Binti, the senior wife hated her and called her *mlaya kidogo* (little whore).

"That night, when the chief fell on the floor, she was filled with terror," Kasubi said. "Yes, the chief asked her if there was *dawa* (poison) in the beer. She was too frightened to speak. She didn't say anything but now she thinks he guessed that there was. He looked stricken, like a child, like a baby. His eyes were red, he spat, then vomited. That's when he died.

"And about the villagers' belief that she used witchcraft, she doesn't know if she had *those* powers that night. She did feel very powerful when she put the powder in the beer because she knew many people wanted her to do this. Then she says she got scared."

At that point Kasubi asked about the chief's son, who gave her the red powder. They talked for quite a while, the sister nodded and poured more tea. Then Welelo grunted and her eyes hardened. Kasubi turned to me and whispered.

"She says the chief's son was a bastard! He used her. He lied to her. He caused her to go to prison. He never helped her, even after she was out of prison. He had promised to be her lover, to make her powerful, but he ran away to Kigoma and took another wife. He is a *fisi* (hyena). He ruined her life."

There were more words and Welelo looked even more disgusted. Suddenly her sister squirmed and covered her own mouth with both hands. "Welelo says he was a very bad lover. He had no stamina. He had a small penis. He couldn't finish her. She hears he is sick in Kigoma. She says 'good.' She hopes he gets sicker. She is glad."

Kasubi looked at me as if to say "That's it." I put my notebook away and got out the little packets of tea and sugar and handed them to Kasubi. He passed them with both hands to Welelo as a small gift, a *zawadi*. She nodded, looked at her sister and the two women went into their hut. Welelo slammed the wooden door hard enough to scare the brown chickens.

As we walked back to the road, Kasubi asked me what I now knew that I didn't know before.

"I think we know that the chief suspected poison. Her answer to that question convinces me the old man died of fright. It's called 'death by suggestion' by anthropologists. I have a friend in Nairobi who will help explain it. I'll let you know."

"Welelo says he was a very bad lover. He had no stamina."

✧

In Kenya a few weeks later I laid out the case for Patrick Ndeka as we sat in his hospital office on a warm, rainy afternoon.

"Sure, an interesting case!" he said. "It's particularly good you got a look at the situation over all these years. Of course we will never know what really killed the chief since there was no autopsy of his body, but it sounds like 'death by suggestion,' also called 'voodoo death.' Pretty common with the Australian aborigines, the 'bone pointing' business."

Ndeka said he wanted to switch topics for a minute, back to our earlier discussions on the reason behind the killings of old women as witches. He remembered the "lifeboat" ideas, with villagers killing "witches" when the economic outlook is bleak and how American economist Edward Miguel had statistically connected the killings to cycles of drought or flooding.[*]

"But there is an even deeper explanation of these killings," he mused. "It has to do with village consensus, the agreement to murder.

* Edward Miguel, "Poverty and Witch Killing." *Review of Economic Studies.* (vol 72, no 4, pp 1153-1172), 2005

A British sociologist, Stanley Cohen, has put his finger on it. Witchcraft persists because of a kind of mass hysteria. He calls it 'moral panic.' It's an idea from his work on street gangs and other groups that get very violent when they perceive their organization is falling apart."

"For us," he continued, "I think Cohen would say that communities here descend into witchcraft-related violence out of abject despair. Their deepest fear is that their community—their culture—is disintegrating. The violence is not really about old ladies as witches, but about losing the most sacred thing humans have—a solid community. The actions are the cumulative effect of drought, famine, plague, or the aftermath of war. These conditions create panic or hysteria and then a frenzied search for scapegoats. When villagers are convinced their culture is collapsing, they can justify horrendous acts to save themselves. It explains all those killings in western Tanzania, your 'Tanzanian Holocaust.' And here in Kenya, in Kisii District, same type of killings."

Before I could say anything, Ndeka put his finger up that he wanted to continue.

"And, hear this," he crowed. "I have found a rare word for the whole process. It's 'senicide,' the killing of elders. It is a kind of 'death hastening.' It went on in traditional cultures, still does I suspect. Old Eskimos left behind on the ice floes. Your early American Hopi, South Africa's San people. Bororos in the Amazon, even early Fijians: all examples of senicide."

I nodded. "Good word for this business. Senicide, the opposite of infanticide, both ways to reduce economic burdens. And both practices can use witchcraft as an excuse. Remember last year, the 'child witches' of the Congo and Zambia, children expelled from their families as witches? Remember those poor kids? At least ten thousand forced into the streets in Kinshasa, as supposed witches."

We both reached for our paper coffee cups and I decided it was time to ask the question that had been bothering me for a long time.

"Why does witchcraft persist? Why does it persist across Bantu Africa when Africans by the millions detest it?"

Ndeka looked at me.

"Why does it persist? You have said it before. Governments can't confront it because too many of our damn leaders are implicated in it.

It's 'senicide,' the killing of elders.

A lot of them use witchcraft to intimidate their opposition. It's economic, it's profitable, it's good copy so our media give witchcraft credibility. The damn tabloids give witchcraft ideas power. The churches use witchcraft. But your little boy, that kid, Ali, he is the real reason, or his teachers are. Most African teachers are too timid or too intimidated to confront it. What were your words? Witchcraft ideas are taught within the family to the point that they become like emotions. Emotion beats reason! That's why it persists. Emotion trumps reason."

When he spoke again, Ndeka was in a totally different world.

"But who are we, anyway?" he asked. "You, my friend Miller, are a western white man. I'm a black—half-African, half western. I grew up with witchcraft, but I don't believe it. We are outsiders looking in. We need to know someone who has been embroiled, who is inside, who sees it through only African eyes. Someone who has been accused of witchcraft."

The rain had stopped and rays of brilliant sun had broken through the dark clouds. We both stared out the window, watching a nurse push an old man in a high-backed wheelchair on the wet sidewalk.

"Let me tell you about a woman I once knew," I said. "Let me tell you about Mohammadi."

10

Mohammadi's Shadow

2004–2005

Salimu Hassani, fisherman, Mbwamaji village, Tanzania
Chief John Mtura Mdeka, age 28, son of Chief Mdeka

Sitting on the edge of his outrigger canoe, digging his toes in the sand and looking out over the shimmering Indian Ocean, Salimu Hassani, the oldest fisherman in Mbwamaji village assured me of three things. All the fishermen still believed witchcraft could affect their fish catches, particularly when fishing at night. And yes, they believed it was still good to fumigate their houses once a year against witchcraft, and yes, traveling witch-finders still came through the village. One named Beppo had just been there. He used dissected baobab fruit in a divination ritual to make sure the village was free of witchcraft.

Judy and I had come from Dar es Salaam, first on the Kivukoni ferry across the harbor, then on the rickety bus down the eighteen miles of sandy road, through the palm trees and sultry air. The trip was to bring photos back to people I had known when I worked there forty years earlier. It was now 2004, and a remarkable number were still alive.

We also planned to return with photographs to villages in western Tanzania. The next week on the little propeller plane from Dar es Salaam to the dirt airstrip in Tabora, I was thumbing through my old field notes when I ran across a section on the trial of Mohammadi. Kabota, my assistant, had heard that she had other relatives in Usagari, aside from her brother, but no one had come to her assistance. The Mohammadi case had remained a mystery because I did not know why she was banished. What was the real story? I decided to try to find out.

At the airstrip my friend Kasubi, whom I had seen the year before, was smiling and waving, even as the backdraft from the propellers covered him in red dust.

"I have sent a message to the new chief of Usagari," he said as we shook hands. "We will meet at 4:00 tomorrow. Get ready to dance—they want to do a traditional welcome."

"But he can't dance," Judy said.

Kasubi, who had just met her, was very polite. "Madam," he said, "they will teach him."

The meeting was to be at the old chief's compound where I had lived years before. Kasubi had access to an ancient Land Rover, and for the price of fuel and the promise of a full tank later we could use it for two days. We drove to the outskirts of Usagari, gathered our photos and gifts and began hiking into the hills. It was a hot, sultry afternoon, the sun to our backs, a stillness in the air. The trail seemed far steeper and more rock-strewn than I remembered.

Faintly, like distant thunder, came the deep booming voices of African drums. I had heard the big ceremonial drums before, but this

Chief's compound. Usagari village, Tanzania, 2004.

time a chill came over me. In a few minutes the sound was echoing across the valley. As our trail rounded a huge stone boulder, the old chief's compound came into view and Kasubi began to bob his head.

"Get ready to dance," he said again. "They are coming for you."

Nearly a dozen women were gyrating up the trail, their ceremonial *fimbo* sticks held out, dancing with the sound of the drums. Some were shuffling, some moving in stutter steps; others with heads thrown back were trilling into the air. Further back at least thirty men danced near the drums. The young chief, dressed in traditional regalia, stood watching us from near a wooden throne.

Three children took our packages, and little ceremonial spears were put into our hands. We were danced up to the booming drums, then around the compound twice and finally to chairs on either side of the chief.

Ali Bakari, whom I had known as a ten-year-old, the grandson of my friend Saidi Bakari, came forward to welcome us on behalf of his dead grandfather. Two elders spoke, then Kasubi spoke and presented

A traditional welcome with drums and dancing for the author and Judy Miller, Usagari village, Tanzania, 2004.

the village with our gifts: thirty-eight packets of tea and thirty-eight small bags of sugar, one for each year I had been away. Two little boys were told to bring a table and arrange them in front of the throne. Judy and I stepped forward and handed a box of photos to the chief.

Chief John opened the box and studied the top picture of his father, who was in the regalia the young chief was now wearing. Without a word he walked to the little ritual hut that was still there. He studied the picture, moved slightly to the left, and then looked at Judy, who was holding the camera.

"Please," he said in perfect English.

There was silence. Children were hushed, several old men bowed their heads, and for a moment the village of Usagari, Tanzania, rolled back the clock. Young John Mturu Mdeka, son of Mdeka, grandson of Mturu (the poisoned one), and distant nephew of Mirambo, the conquerer of western Tanzania, then strode back to his throne, sat down, opened another box of pictures, and motioned the elders to come and look over his shoulder.

Villagers with Chief John Mdeka, Judy and Norman Miller, Usagari, Tanzania, 2004.

Judy and I watched as men who had survived the intervening years crowded around the chief, their gnarled hands holding pictures of themselves as young men. As the grandchildren pushed in and strained to see the images, there were "ohs" and "ahs," then silent moments as people saw those who had died. When they had gone through a box, the chief motioned for it to be taken to the women clustered nearby.

The next day Kasubi, Chief John and I sat with five of the elders and talked about the intervening years. A new all-weather road allowed Usagari charcoal makers on bicycles to get to Tabora in two hours. There was a new well, a new primary school and a tiny clinic with two beds—one of them a maternity bed I had brought to the village the year before. The main *duka* was still run by the Omani Arab family that had been there thirty-eight years ago. It was now set back from the new road but it was still the main trade center for kerosene, rope, sugar, dried fruit and salt.

The elders tried to paint a picture of progress but, in fact, there had been little change. Few children had shoes and some showed signs of malnutrition. Most gardens were overgrown with weeds, and only a few

chickens or ducks could be seen. There were still only two tea houses, the political party office was still padlocked and the village executive officer lived elsewhere. Most telling, there were very few young people in the village.

Plenty of evidence did exist, however, that witchcraft was a day-to-day reality. In the 1980s, the United Nations had opened a camp for Burundian refugees in Ulyankulu, sixteen miles up the road, and there was now a settlement there of several thousand people. Most of the medicines and witchcraft protection devices in Usagari now came from the Burundian refugees who had convinced the entire region that their devices—including some from the eastern Congo—were more powerful.

Chinese mineral prospectors had found veins of gold beyond Ulyankulu, and some Usagari villagers were trying their luck as miners, as they had in the past. It was still a dangerous business because the deep open trenches could easily cave in and bury the miner. These accidents were widely believed to be caused by witchcraft, and different kinds of protection charms were sold in the village.

HIV/AIDS had taken hold and the village paramedic told me most villagers believed it was caused by witchcraft, or that witches were the ones infected. Both the local healers, who now had certificates from the Tanzania Traditional Healers Assocation, quietly admitted to Kasubi that witchcraft was their most common diagnosis and that they treated HIV/AIDS with pain killers.

When talking to the elders, however, it was Mohammadi that I most wanted to ask about. Was there anything more to learn about the trial of the woman whose dead child had come to haunt her on moonless nights? Now, with the young chief, we were again sitting under

Photos left: Changes in the author's village, Usagari, Tanzania, include the (A) Old road, (1965) and the (B) Same road in 2005. (C) Chief Mtura Mdeka and senior wife (1965). (D) His son, John Mtura Mdeka in 2005, both photos taken at the same ritual house near the chief's compound. (E) The Omani Arab family who operated the Usagari general store in 1965, and (F) with the author and S. Kasubi in 2005. (Author's collection)

the same mango tree, almost in the place where her trial was held. I thought back to the men on their little stools, the women hoeing in the background, Mohammadi and her brother staring at the ground.

When I asked about the trial, only one old man said he vaguely remembered her, but that there had been several such cases in his lifetime. With Kasubi translating, I gently tried to jog his memory. "Don't you remember? The woman Mohammadi was accused of witchcraft because some of you thought she went out naked at night, howling and making strange sounds."

He stared at me through thick, Coke-bottle glasses.

"Don't you remember?" I persisted. "I think you were the one who said she controlled insects and sent flies into the nose of the baby who died. Didn't you say she spilled water on purpose in times of water shortage, and even could transform herself into a hyena. All of you decided she was unbalanced and bad for the neighborhood. She could cause pregnancies to fail and children to die."

No one spoke. The old man with thick glasses stared blankly at me. He seemed distracted, almost drugged, frozen in place. At that point Kasubi leaned forward and touched my elbow. "He does not want to remember," Kasubi whispered.

I thought about Peter Rigby years ago at the Dodoma hotel. Rigby had assured me that everyone remembered William Hanning, the geologist who had been speared to death as a witch. They denied it because no one was allowed to remember witches. No one dared talk about them.

Chief John seemed to sense my hope to close the story.

"What is it you really want to know, Bwana Norman?" he asked politely.

"Is there anything that explains why she was banished? Is there a deeper story," I asked.

Chief John looked at Kasubi and then spoke quietly in Nyamwezi to the man in the Coke-bottle glasses, gently laying his hand on the elder's knee. Slowly the old man began to nod, and then to speak in a whisper to the young chief.

"He remembers some things," Kasubi translated. "In fact, he admits that he himself was related to Mohammadi. He was her cousin."

The three men talked at length, then Kasubi turned to me.

"OK… Mohammadi's father was a herbalist in Ibiri. He was beaten and nearly killed for practising witchcraft. His activities had been rumored for a long time—that he used poisons on people and sold poisons. It was a very serious case. This elder here with the thick glasses says the herbalist was banished to Uwoya when Mohammadi was a little girl…eleven or twelve at the time. Because her father was a condemned witch, she was unmarriageable. She lost value. No man would pay the bride-price because her father was a witch."

He coughed and cleared his throat. "She was finally married off to an old man…he paid only a few shillings. He died soon after they had a baby girl."

Kasubi nodded to the elder, thanking him for the information.

"In his view," I asked, "was Mohammadi really a witch?"

More words were exchanged.

"He doesn't know, Norman. All he knows is that Mohammadi had other relatives around here, right here in Usagari. She had kinship ties to four other families, and of course to her brother. They all wanted her banished—including the brother."

"Her brother?" I exclaimed. "What a bastard, he pretended such loyalty. What about the others, her family members? Why didn't they help her?"

"It is pretty simple," Kasubi said after he again spoke to the old man. "Mohammadi was causing suspicion to fall on all of them. This is a small community. They were afraid of being accused. She was hurting their reputations, making their lives hard. Secretly her brother agreed that she be banished."

We sat there in silence. "Finally, we get the inside story," I said as Kasubi turned to me with a resigned look on his face.

"Let it go now, Norman. You are the only one who wants to remember her. Not these old men…they don't want to remember. There have been too many witches. They want to forget her now."

Two days later, as we flashed by the terminal with Kasubi frantically waving goodbye, our little plane lifted into the air and the dry, rolling panorama of western Tanzania came into view. I could see the dirt road to Usagari, and then for a few moments, the village itself. As I craned my neck, Usagari, Tanzania, grew smaller and smaller, and then it was only a dot on the horizon. Curiously, at that very moment the plane's shadow began chasing us across the savannah. For a moment it looked like a woman carrying water from a well.

Epilogue: The Future of Witchcraft

In the years since 2004 when Mohammadi's shadow chased our little airplane across the savanna I have only been back to East Africa once. The trip was to work with African friends in all three countries, to find ways to control religious violence, particularly the witchcraft-based atrocities. We were also concerned more broadly about witchcraft violence in the "born again" Christian churches and in some of the extreme Islamic sects in East Africa. There had been several incidents, including two major bomb attacks.

The plan was first to do field research in the three countries and then meet to propose new policy ideas for the governments. We thought the problems were compelling: violence against women and the elderly, defilement and witchcraft-related child abuse—all serious human rights and social justice issues. A foundation was interested in funding the project. We wanted to design a village-level "stop witchcraft" program that involved teachers, healers, religious leaders, plus local government and non-governmental agency workers. We thought there was something to learn from the anti-witchcraft policies developed in Ghana and South Africa. Because it was a cross-border project we needed the approval of all three governments, through their ministries of education or external affairs. Because the violence surrounding witchcraft is well known, we were certain they would agree.

They didn't. The first hint of trouble came when the Makerere-based group in Uganda was told it was "too political and potentially embarrassing." The Kenyan government did not respond to our repeated requests and even when the support of the Tanzanian government was clear, the university researchers became nervous about their political "exposure" and fell to arguing about procedural details.

Meanwhile, new witchcraft-based violence surfaced. In Tanzania an epidemic of albino killings spread across the southern part of the country, then into Zambia and Kenya.* In Uganda, an outbreak of homophobia was fanned when homosexuals were equated with witches. The Ugandan Parliament debated a bill for the execution of homosexuals, which was shelved only after world-wide protests. In Kenya, witchcraft killings and village-level witch-hunts continued in both the coastal and Kisii regions.

When our project fell apart, I went to see Charles Ndeka, my friend who had helped develop some of the project. He was not surprised.

"Too sensitive a topic" he said with a wry smile. "These governments can't let that cat out of the bag. Too many political leaders would be implicated, too many politicians use juju threats to get elected."

As he had done so often, Ndeka sat back and put his feet up on the desk. His mood was somber. He seemed to sense what I was about to say.

"It's an on-going tragedy out there," I protested. "All across Africa millions of people detest witchcraft, and cry out against it. Yet they are victimized, often in their home village, usually by neighbors or kinfolk. Women, elder men, even children! When does it end, Charles, when does it end?"

We looked at each other. There was a flicker of hope in his eyes.

"Look," he said, "I think we Africans will eventually beat witchcraft, at least the more violent witch hunts. How? By education, by ending the deep poverty. But the fundamental superstitions? The irrational beliefs among the less educated? That is something else." He paused for a long time.

"Tell me, Norman. When will these things end in your country?"

*The atrocities were based on the old ideas of *sympathetic magic*, in these cases that skin or body parts from an albino person could bring good luck and protect against witchcraft. The killings became so bad that the Tanzanian government appointed a prominent albino woman to the President's cabinet to lead the education and prevention campaigns. Also between 2009-2012 similar cases of murder, in these cases child-murder, erupted in Uganda. These were also based on *sympathetic magic* ideas that such ritual sacrifices could lead to the acquiring of great wealth. The government's investigative reports blamed the thinking on witchcraft.

Further Reading and Bibliography

For the reader who wishes to go beyond a memoir about witchcraft into other kinds of literature, there is a great deal to feast upon. An excellent historical introduction to the topic is Wolfgang Behringer's *Witches and Witch-Hunts*, as is another broadguage study of political power and the manipulation of supernatural ideas by Stephen Ellis and Gerrie Ter Haar, entitled *Worlds of Power*. For the history of witchcraft, both in Europe and early America, books by Hugh Trevor-Roper and John Demos, cited below, are excellent starting places. Lucy Mair's *Witchcraft*, although dated, is still a valuable introduction. to the literature on witchcraft, as is a book by Henrietta Moore and Todd Saunders on witchcraft in post-colonial Africa.

Anthropological studies about witchcraft begin with E.E. Evans-Pritchard for Africa, and Clyde Kluckholm for Native American. Overall, anthropologists have done a great deal of work on the topic, much of it focused on specific ethnic groups. Examples include books by Peter Geschiere, Jean and John Comaroff, Elias Bongmba, and Max Marwick. Specifically for East Africa, there is a collection of studies organized by John Middleton and E.H. Winter entitled *Witchcraft and Sorcery in East Africa*. John Mbiti's *African Religions and Philosophy* places witchcraft ideas in Africa's broader belief system. Ivan Karp's *Exploring African Systems of Thought* provides a similar service. Adam Asforth and Isak Niehaus provide a political perspective on witchcraft in the South African context. The work of Edward Miguel, cited in the memoir, offers an important economic perspective. Texts by Monica Visona and Rosalind Hackett are a beginning for those interested in the relations between religion and African art. The books cited below provide a general introduction to the topic and are not intended to be exhaustive.

Ashforth, Adam. *Madumo, A Man Bewitched.* Chicago: University of Chicago Press, 2000.

Behringer, Wolfgang. *Witches and Witch-Hunts.* Cambridge, U.K. and Malden, Mass.: Polity Press, 2004.

Bond, George Clement and Diane M. Ciekawy, eds. *Witchcraft Dialogues: Anthropological and Philosophical Exchanges.* Athens, Ohio: Ohio University Press, 2001.

Bongmba, Elias. *African Witchcraft and Otherness: A Philosophical and Theological Critique of Intersubjective Relations.* Albany: SUNY Press, 2001.

Comaroff, Jean, and John Comaroff, eds. *Modernity and Its Malcontents: Ritual and Power in Postcolonial Africa.* Chicago: University of Chicago Press, 1993.

Demos, John. *The Enemy Within: 2,000 Years of Witch-hunting in the Western World.* New York: Viking, 2008.

Demos, John. *Entertaining Satan: Witchcraft and the Culture of Early New England.* New York: Oxford University Press, 1982.

Ellis, Stephen, and Gerrie Ter Haar. *Worlds of Power: Religious Thought and Political Practice in Africa.* New York: Oxford University Press, 2004.

Evans-Pritchard, Edward Evan. *Witchcraft, Oracles and Magic among the Azande.* Oxford: Oxford University Press, 1937.

Geschiere, Peter. *The Modernity of Witchcraft: Politics and the Occult in Postcolonial Africa,* Charlottesville, VA: University Press of Virginia, 1997.

Green, Maia. *Priests, Witches and Power.* Caimbridge: Caimbridge University Press, 2003.

Hackett, Rosalind I.J. *Art and Religion in Africa.* London: Cassell, 1996.

Karp, Ivan, and Charles S. Bird, eds. *Explorations in African Systems of Thought.* Bloomington, Indiana: Indiana University Press, 1980.

Kluckhohn, Clyde. *Navaho Witchcraft.* Boston: Beacon Press, 1944.

Luongo, Katherine A. *Witchcraft and Colonial Rule in Kenya, 1900-1955.* Cambridge: Cambridge University Press, 2011.

Mair, Lucy: *Witchcraft.* New York: McGraw-Hill Book Company: World University Library, 1969.

Marwick, Max, ed. *Witchcraft and Sorcery: Selected Readings,* second edition. New York: Penguin Books, 1982.

Mbiti, John S. *African Religions and Philosophy.* London, Heinemann, 1969.

Miguel, Edward. "Poverty and Witch Killing", *Review of Economic Studies,* 2005, vol. 72, no. 4, pp.1153–1172.

Middleton, John, ed. *Magic, Witchcraft and Curing.* Austin, TX: University of Texas Press, 1977.

Middleton, John, and E. H. Winter, eds. *Witchcraft and Sorcery in East Africa.* London: Routledge and Kegan Paul, 1963, 2004.

Moore, Henrietta, and Todd Sanders, eds. *Magical Interpretations, Material Realities: Modernity, Witchcraft and the Occult in Postcolonial Africa.* New York: Routledge, 2001.

Niehaus, Isak, and Eliazaar Mohlala, Kally Shokane. *Witchcraft, Power and Politics: Exploring the Occult in the South African Lowveld.* Sterling, VA: Pluto Press, 2001.

Pares, Luis Nicolau and Roger Sansi, editors. *Sorcery in the Black Atlantic.* Chicago: University of Chicago Press, 2011.

Ter Haar, Gerrie. editor. *Imagining Evil: Witchcraft Beliefs and Accusations in Contemporary Africa.* Trenton, NJ: Africa World Press, 2007.

Trevor-Roper, Hugh R. *The European Witch-Craze of the Sixteenth and Seventeenth Centuries.* New York: Penguin, 1969.

Visona, Monica Blackmun, Robin Poynor, and Herbert M. Cole. *A History of Art in Africa,* second edition. Upper Saddle River, NJ: Pearson: Prentice Hall, 2008.

Acknowledgments and Credits

My longest standing debt in the creation of this book is to my African neighbors and teachers, people in villages and market towns called Usagari, Sesso and Maneramango in Tanzania, Nyere, Ukunda and Marsabit in Kenya and Kisoro and Kabale in Uganda. These " thank yous" stretch back more than four decades and include most of the names mentioned at the head of each chapter. In particular, Simeon Maseki, an anthropologist at the University of Dar es Salaam has been a mentor on issues of witchcraft.

Outside Africa, my greatest debt is to a Scotsman, Duncan MacDonald, a gifted thinker, philosopher, physican and former "flying doctor" in Zambia. Our discussions and our friendship also go back more than four decades.

The final production of a book like this demand talents which I do not have. Happily they were found in a wonderful editor, Susan Ludmer-Gliebe, in the additional editorial skills of Jean Lawe and Ruth Sylvester, and, in the graphic design genius of Carrie Fradkin. Eden Abram and Susan Whelihan, both talented artists gave my very rough sketches new life. Ellen Kozak, plus Peter Allen at the Evans Map Room, at Dartmouth College created the maps from my sketches. Most recently Sarah Welsch and Dennis Grady have brought superb publishing advice to the project, as has Chad Finer, a talented photographer. Two Reference Librarians at Dartmouth, Amy Witzel and Francis Oscadal have helped me for longer than any of us can remember.

I am also indebted to several institutions that have provided illustrative material, particularly the British Museum in London, and the Hood Museum at Dartmouth in Hanover, New Hampshire. The national museums in Kenya and Tanzania have also been valuable sources, as has the *Daily Nation* (Nairobi), the *Tanzania Standard*, (Dar es Salaam), and the *Argus* and *Monitor* in Kampala, Uganda. Each are acknowledged with thanks.

Any project of this nature is based on the long term support of an inner circle, those who been there to discuss ideas and to offer advice. In this case they are Rodger Yeager, Larry Hausman, John Thompson, James Greene, James Strickler, Judge Philip Ransley (Kenya), and in the inner, inner circle, Judith, Scott and Amy Miller.

Photo Credits

Most of the photos in the book are from my own collection with the exception of those listed below. For these I have either secured permission or await responses to my request for the right to print the photo. Please contact Post Office Box 333, Norwich, Vermont, 05055, USA.

Page 2, 13 ARTstor Digital Library, Dartmouth College
Page 13 Courtesy, Poznan Museum, Poznan,Poland.
Page 18 Courtesy, National Museum, Dar es Salaam, Tanzania,
Page 24 J. Gus Liebenow Collection, Indiana University
Page 27 Larry Hausman Collection, McLean,Virginia
Page 28 Corbis Images, HU 055559
Page 53 Courtesy Kenya Ministry of Information
Page 84-5 Courtesy British Museum, AF/A 44-137-139
Page 86 Hans Cory Collection, University of Dar es Salaam *
Page 87 Photos A-E, Hans Cory Collection, above
Page 87 Photo F. Private Collection,
Page 87 Photo G. Jesper Kirknaes, Copenhagen Denmark
Page 89 Author's sketches courtesy of Barrie Reynolds, Rhodes-Livingstone Museum, Zambia. **
Page 93 Courtesy British Museum, AF/B 19/35
Page 94 Author's sketches courtesy of Barrie Reynolds
Page 96 Author's sketches from British Museum displays
Page 96 Used by permission of the owner.
Page 97 Courtesy Uganda Museum, Kampala, (requested)***
Page 112 Courtesy Dailey Nation, Nairobi, Kenya
Page 113 Courtesy Charles Good, Jr. Collection (photo A)
Page 113 Courtesy Dailey Nation, Nairobi, Kenya (photos B-D)_
Page 115 Courtesy East African Standard, Nairobi, Kenya
Page 134 Courtesy M. Daneel, Boston University
Page 165 Courtesy Frank McEwen collection (photos A,C,F)
Page 166 Courtesy Peter Mulindwa, Kampala, Uganda (requested)
Page 183 Courtesy Kenya Ministry of Information
Page 187 Reuters Pictures/JonathonWright. GF2E66716BSo1

References

* Cory, Hans, Wall-paintings by Snake Charmers in Tanganyika. New York: Grove Press, 1953. (99 pps, mural paintings and decoration, LCCN 53000982, OCLC AEO 145LB)
**Reynolds, Barrie, Magic Divination and Witchcraft Among the Barotse of Northern Rhodesia. London: Chatto and Windus, 1963
*** Sekintu, C.M.and K.P Wachsmann, Wall Patterns in Hima Huts, Kampala, Uganda: The Uganda Museum, Paper no. 1, 1956.

Index